WITHDRAWN

Napoleon

DATE DUE			
JUN 2 9 1988			

H. A. L. FISHER

Herbert Albert Laurens

Napoleon

OXFORD UNIVERSITY PRESS
London Oxford New York

Oxford University Press
OXFORD LONDON NEW YORK
GLASGOW NEW YORK TORONTO MELBOURNE WELLINGTON
CAPE TOWN SALISBURY IBADAN NAIROBI LUSAKA ADDIS ABABA
BOMBAY CALCUTTA MADRAS KARACHI LAHORE DACCA
KUALA LUMPUR SINGAPORE HONG KONG TOKYO

© OXFORD UNIVERSITY PRESS 1967

Bibliography

First published in the Home University Library *1912*
First issued as an Oxford University Press paperback 1967
This reprint 1969

PRINTED IN GREAT BRITAIN BY THE CAMELOT PRESS LTD, LONDON AND SOUTHAMPTON

Contents

Maps

1
Youth

As we think of Napoleon Bonaparte what a world of visions and memories rises before the mind! Who does not know the outward form of the greatest conqueror and captain of modern times: the small, almost dwarfish, figure, the rounded symmetry of the head, the pale olive cheek and massive brow, the nose and lips carved as it were from the purest marble of the antique world, and above all the deep-set eyes of lustrous grey, now flashing with electric fires, now veiled in impenetrable contemplation? The set of his figure is familiar too, as are the clothes in which it had been the delight of painters to portray him. We know the compact energy of his chest and shoulders, the flashing impetuosity of each gesture and movement, the white teeth and delicate hands, and the little cocked hat and long coat of grey in which he was used to ride to victory. Who has not seen him in print and picture, the gaunt young hero of the Republic charging with the flag at Arcole, the Emperor kneeling before the altar of Notre Dame in the long and sumptuous robes of his coronation, the grim leader of a haggard cavalcade treading the deadly snows of a Russian winter, the cloaked figure upon a ship's deck with huddled shoulders and sunken chin and a far-off look of tragedy in his set and melancholy gaze? And the thoughts and feelings which glow into consciousness at the sound of this illustrious name are every whit as varied and chequered as the outward events of his life seen through the imagination of the painter. Perhaps in the whole range of history no one has aroused emotions so opposite and so intense or within his own lifetime has claimed so much of the admiration, the fear, and the hatred of mankind. Even the colder critics of posterity view his course not only with mixed and blended judgements, but with a kind of bewilderment at the union in one life and character of so much grandeur and roguery, gold and alloy. For those to whom psychological analysis is wearisome he stands simply as the miraculous man of action, who without assistance of wealth or station mounted to the highest pinnacle of human fortune, supplying by the weight of one transcendent example a conclusive answer to the theory that the art and mystery of politics is an esoteric thing, a perquisite of pedigrees and privilege. The man of whom Madame de Staël said that 'of all the inheritance of his terrible power there remained only to the human race the deadly knowledge of some further secrets in the art of tyranny', is also the child of the Revolution, the most dazzling proof of his own democratic doctrine that in every society a career should be open to talent. And so long as men go to the past for the pathos and romance of great vicissitudes of fortune, or for the serious interest of feats of statesmanship, or for documents of human power and resolve, or for the more elusive secrets of the passionate temperament, or else that they may win an insight into the human forces which move the world, they will continue to study the life of Napoleon, and to find in it at the very least a story as wonderful as those of the giants and fairies, and at the most the greatest explosion of human energy which in modern times has altered the politics of civilized man.

He was born at Ajaccio on August 15, 1769, the second son of Charles-Marie Bonaparte and Marie-Letizia Ramolino. His paternal stem drew its root from Florence (branches of it have been traced at Sarzana and San Miniato in Tuscany), but ever since 1529 the ancestors of Napoleon had been settled in Corsica. Here in this lovely scene of rugged mountains and dark chestnut forests and azure spaces of sky and sea the Bonapartes flourished in the esteem of their simple neighbours. Proud of its patrician origin, the family, though far from wealthy, was by the standard of that rude and primitive society reckoned to be the most prosperous in Ajaccio. Five Bonapartes served at different times on the island council. But the evidence of ancestral ability is stronger on the maternal than on the father's side. The father of Napoleon was handsome, intelligent, with a not uncommon Italian turn for poetry and rhetoric, but extravagant and restless, constantly embarrassed for money, and driven to every kind of ingenious solicitation and shift to obtain it. His mother Letizia was a woman in a thousand. Far into old age she retained the beauty of face

pro - napo   romantic?

and dignity of carriage which were hers by right of nature, and which would have won her admiration in any company in the world. Her mind was plain and unfurnished. To the end of her life she could neither pronounce nor speak the French language without ridiculous mistakes, and her economies were carried to the point of avarice; but her character was solid as a rock of granite, and as she had faced adversity with courage, so she was neither changed nor spoiled by the marvellous revolution in her fortunes. In 1793 Paoli addressed her as Cornelia, meaning that this shrewd, resolute, and beautiful country-woman was fit to bear a progeny of heroes.

In the middle of the eighteenth century it was a title of honour to be a native of Corsica. Every lover of liberty had followed with sympathy the gallant struggle which the inhabitants of that small and freedom-loving island had waged, first against the odious rule of Genoa, and then against the powerful monarchy of France. The name of Pasquale Paoli, the hero of the War of Independence, the leader and law-giver of his people, was famous in every capital in Europe, and the characteristics of a country so remote, and apparently by reason of that remoteness retaining the large and simple heroism of classical times, was matter for the curiosity of travellers and politicians. Europe thought of Corsica then, as she has thought since of Greece and other small nations struggling for independence. And the youth of Napoleon, born in the very year in which Corsica finally passed under the dominion of France, was filled with the reverbera-tion of that island epic. Stories of the strokes and hazards of the patriotic war must have been everywhere around him. He learned to know how his father had drafted a proclamation to the Corsican people, and how just before his birth his mother was driven out into the woods and mountains to share the perils of the patriot army. The star of his youth was Paoli. His dream was, now to write the history of his island, now to effect its liberation from the French.

The Corsican bore a character for sobriety, courage, and hardihood. Hate was for him a virtue, vengeance a duty, pardon an infamy. He felt the call of the clan like a Highlander, an Albanian, or a Zulu, and was full of the pride and self-assurance common to gallant men who have never met a superior. Vigilant and astute in his judgement of character, he was a master of dissimulation save where passion broke in and spoiled the reckoning. His standard of honour forbade theft, enjoined hospitality, and tolerated woman as the drudge of the

household and the field. In general his deportment was noted as
grave and stoical. He was sparing of amusement, would sit at cards
without a word and suffer torture without a cry; but when the seal
of silence was once broken, language would stream from him like a
torrent, an index of that uneasy, impatient, quarrelsome energy
which was a common attribute of the race. In these and other
particulars of temperament Napoleon Bonaparte was a true Corsican.

The main part of Napoleon's education was conducted not in Corsica
but in France. For seven years and nine months he never set eyes upon
his home or upon his mother. When he left Ajaccio on December 15,
1778, to embark on the study of the French language at Autun, he
was a child of nine; when he returned upon leave in September 1786
he was seventeen years old and a sub-lieutenant in a regiment of
artillery. Yet absence had rather quickened than dimmed the fervour
of his patriotism. As a schoolboy at Brienne, and again at the military
school in Paris, he felt himself an exile in an enemy's country, using a
foreign tongue and compelled to associate with boys who despised
him for his alien accent, his lean purse, and his lack of influential
connexions. The sense of isolation drove him inwards on himself. As
a little child he had been quarrelsome and turbulent; he was now
taciturn, morose, unpopular with his fellows, 'dry as parchment', in
his own words, but secretly tormented by the flames of ambition.
Linguistic capacity he never possessed, but from childhood he had
shown an aptitude and taste for mathematics which was further
developed by his French instructors. His father had originally
designed him for the navy, but the project was changed, perhaps at
the boy's desire, before the five years' course at Brienne was concluded, and it was decided that he should enter the artillery, being
that branch of the profession of arms in which brains and industry
might most easily balance the lack of outward advantages. He had
given early proof of military tastes; as he trotted down to his little
school at Ajaccio he would exchange his breakfast of white bread for
the coarse brown rations of the barrack, saying that he must prepare
to lead the life of a soldier.

The evidence with regard to his intellectual and moral development at this period of life, though not abundant, is decisive in
quality. His letters written from school are serious, lucid, and
practical. At fourteen he summed up the character of his elder brother
Joseph, and decided that being too frivolous for the army, he should

certainly be sent into the Church. At fifteen and a half, learning of the death of his father, he wrote with a precocious sense of civic service: 'Our country has lost a keen, enlightened, and honest citizen. It was so decreed by the Supreme Being.' We are tempted to ask whether he was ever young. It is clear that even as a schoolboy he viewed the profession of arms, not as an occasion for brilliant spectacles, but as that branch of science complete mastery of which, only to be achieved by devouring industry, was the secret of political greatness. History and geography were his absorbing passions. He would imagine himself one of Plutarch's heroes, and he found his first incitement to ambition in that famous *Discourse upon Universal History* in which Bossuet unrolls the succession of the Empires.

On October 28, 1785, Napoleon left the military school in Paris to join the artillery regiment of La Fère which was quartered at Valence. He was then a youth of sixteen years, poor, friendless, destitute of any kind of influence likely to promote his fortunes in the army. His father was dead, and Marbœuf and Boucheporn, the French officials in Corsica who had hitherto forwarded the interests of the family, were dead also. His mother was in great straits for money, and his own pay as sub-lieutenant amounted to seventeen-and-sixpence a week. In the normal course of events six years would elapse before he became a full lieutenant, twelve years before he became a captain; in middle life he might find himself retired on half-pay with hardly enough to keep body and soul together. The grey horizon only steeled his character. Frugality was his second nature, and with no opportunities for vulgar dissipation he plunged the deeper into the world of study. 'Even when I had nothing to do,' he confessed afterwards, 'I vaguely thought that I had no time to lose.'

There was at that time in France a body of prose literature more certain and magisterial in its direction, more seductive in its rich combination of hopefulness, sentiment, and wit, and therefore more cogent in its sway over the generous impulses of youth, than any which Europe had yet known. The French philosophers of the eighteenth century preached the doctrines of reason and humanity to a country swiftly rising to a consciousness that the institutions under which it lived were the relics of a barbarous and superstitious age. They attacked every part of the existing order of society, invoking the widest principles, asking the gravest questions, and exhibiting, as against the darkness and confusion of the present, the dazzling vision of a world governed by the simple rules of rational arithmetic. To this literature of humanism and revolt men of every type and temperament contributed their quota: Voltaire his easy learning and nimble wit, Turgot his grave and philosophic statesmanship, Raynal his gift of angry declamation, Rousseau an incomparable facility for translating into musical French the confessions of a sensitive nature and the ideals of a logical mind. To an impecunious sub-lieutenant of artillery, not wholly absorbed in the technical study of his craft, contact with writers such as these was a liberal education, and in his lonely garret Bonaparte devoured the writings of the philosophers. At seventeen he was a passionate admirer of Rousseau and of Raynal, and attuned, if not to expect, at least to welcome, a political revolution in France.

During his first seven years in the army Napoleon enjoyed large and fruitful opportunities for reading. His military duties were light, his furloughs frequent and prolonged, and he had that exquisite passion for acquisition which comes once only with the first unfolding of intellectual power. 'I have no resources here but work,' he wrote to his mother in 1788. 'I sleep very little since my illness. I go to bed at ten, I rise at four, I have only one meal a day, at three o'clock.' From the philosophers he learnt to despise monks, to hate kings, and to disbelieve in the doctrines of the Christian religion; but philosophy was neither his most congenial study nor the true formative influence in his life. His mind was of the positive, not of the metaphysical order. He revelled in facts and figures, analysing in detail books of history, geography, and travel, that he might understand the political conditions of the world in which he lived. His early copybooks show how painstaking he could be in the tedious drudgery of accumulation. Yet the appetite for the concrete coexisted with spiritual sensibilities of a different order, not only with those which specially belong to youth, such as the delighted acquiescence in vague ideas and indefinite emotions, but with others more purposive and ministerial to action. Romantic dreams of greatness, passionately imagined, mingled with the striving to be literal, to be free from clouds, and to see men and things through plain glass. Ossian and Werther touched him with a sense of the illimitable; Corneille and Racine by their finished portraits of civic greatness. In history he found not only an encyclopaedia of important facts, but 'the base of the moral sciences, the torch of truth, the destroyer of prejudice'. Though he practised his pen on essays and novelettes, his principal ambition was to be the historian of his native land, to exhibit the tyranny against which she had heroically struggled, and of which she was still the reluctant victim. In 1787 he began to compose some Letters on Corsica, and later on made collections at Ajaccio for an elaborate history of the island.

The Revolution which broke out in the spring of 1789 opened sudden and indefinite prospects of advancement of all the poor and disinherited in France. Bonaparte's thoughts flew to Corsica; he would help to free his countrymen from the odious yoke of the French bureaucracy. In September 1789 he obtained a furlough, and with his elder brother Joseph plunged into the whirlpool of the Corsican revolution. He declaimed in the clubs, composed hot revolutionary addresses, and helped to organize a national guard. At Ajaccio, a town of fisher-folk, he was the soul of the opposition to the priests and aristocrats. In 1790 he succeeded, by means even then judged to be unscrupulous, in securing his election as second-in-command of a battalion of Corsican volunteers, an appointment not held to be incompatible with his French commission, and giving him an insight into the leadership and discipline of irregular troops. Meanwhile his view of the political situation was altered by the abolition (November 30, 1789) of crown colony government in Corsica, and by the recognition of the island as a department of the new democratic monarchy of France. From that moment, though his interests were still mainly Corsican, his aversion for France was diminished. The Revolutionary Assembly had acknowledged the merits of his countrymen, had permitted Paoli to return, and had arranged for the due representation of Corsica in the parliamentary system to be created in France. But Napoleon was not destined to be ruler of the goatherds and shepherds of his native hills. As war broke out upon the Continent and as the government in Paris passed more and more under Jacobin dominion Paoli, himself a constitutional monarchist, who had owed much to English hospitality, fell under suspicion as a moderate, an Anglophile, and a traitor. An expedition to Maddalena, a little island off the coast of Sardinia, miscarried owing to a naval mutiny; but in the opinion of some the failure was due to a lukewarmness shading into treachery on the part of the Dictator of Corsica. Lucien Bonaparte, then a fiery young democrat of eighteen summers, having failed to become Paoli's secretary, discovered that he was a traitor, and informed the Jacobins of Toulon that the national hero of Corsica was fit for the guillotine. The Government in Paris accepted without examination the idle word of a young incendiary, decreed (April 2, 1793) Paoli's arrest, and ordered the three Commissioners of the Convention who were at Bastia to effect it. The news of this insult to a man who, for more than a generation, had been regarded as the father of his country, set all Corsica in flame; and surrounded by his faithful herdsmen the old General in his mountain fortress at Corte defied the French Government to do its worst. The island was upon the point of civil war, and the position of the Bonapartes, fatally compromised by the rash action of Lucien and surrounded by the fervent Paolists of Ajaccio, became at once extremely critical.

Napoleon had by this time outgrown his early enthusiasm for the French Revolution. He had passed the summer of 1792 in Paris, had watched the invasion of the Tuileries on June 20, and the massacre of the Swiss guards on August 10. His sense of soldierly discipline was outraged by the spectacle of a mob running riot, and of a regular force hacked to pieces for the want of a prompt and regular leader. 'What cowards!' he exclaimed to his friend Bourrienne, as the crowd streamed into the royal palace on June 20: 'How could they let in this rabble! Why don't they sweep off four or five hundred of them with the cannon! The rest would scamper home fast enough.' In the midst of the revolting slaughter of August 10 he went down into the Tuileries gardens, and with the superb phrase, 'Man of the South, let us save this unfortunate', stayed a Marseillais at his butcher's work. Such scenes as these cured him of his last ideal illusions. He wrote home that the Jacobins were lunatics, that the wheel of State was turned by a pack of vile intriguers, and that the people, viewed at close quarters, was unworthy of the efforts expended in courting its favour. From the distractions and fever of the Terror he found a refuge in 'the sublime science' of astronomy.

Returning to Corsica in the autumn with a captain's rank, Napoleon learned that his family stood in the shade of Paoli's displeasure. The uncrowned King of Corsica had done nothing to help, and therefore had done much to hinder, the candidature of Joseph for the French Convention. He was in truth a Republican of the old school, doubtful of these Jacobinical young Bonapartes, who were in league with suspected or declared enemies. Nevertheless Napoleon continued to cultivate relations with the man who still claimed the allegiance of the better part of the island. He commanded the artillery in the unfortunate expedition to Maddalena, and when the news came to Ajaccio that the arrest of Paoli was decreed, he composed an address to the Convention, protesting in warm and generous terms against so flagrant an injustice to a great and honourable patriot. But the struggle which had now begun in Corsica was too fierce to be assuaged by a pamphlet, however vigorous. The Bonapartes were known to be friends of Salicetti, the French Commissioner at Bastia, and were therefore counted as the foes of Paoli; and Lucien's crowning act of insolence, becoming bruited at Corte, precluded any chance of reconciliation. It came to an open and unequal war. How Napoleon was taken by the Paolists in the mountain village of Bocognano; how he escaped down the long valley to a place of hiding in Ajaccio, and thence again by sea to the north; how, soon after, his mother was waked up at midnight and, with four children, safely drawn from the angry town to the lovely olive groves of Milelli, and thence upon news of Paolist bands across the fragrant hills to the tower of Capitello on the gulf; how the Paolists wreaked their vengeance on the offending clan, pillaging or burning six Bonaparte houses, two gardens, and a mill; and how, finally, after many escapes and wanderings, a boat sailed from Calvi harbour on June 10, 1793, carrying Napoleon and his family away from their native shores and three days later landed the homeless fugitives at Toulon—all this may be found in many books, or may be still learned from the lips of hillmen among the granite homesteads of Corsica.

That summer marked a crisis in the destiny of France. The royalists were up in arms in the west, the Girondins in Normandy, Bordeaux, Marseilles. A serious revolt broke out in Lyons. The Allies recovered Belgium, drove the French from their capital frontier posts, Condé, Mainz, Valenciennes, and threatened an advance into the heart of the country. On August 28, 1793, Toulon, the great military port in the Mediterranean, received a British fleet and hoisted the flag of Louis XVII. At no time was the unity of France or the preservation of the republican government so gravely imperilled. For honest and moderate men the course of duty was by no means clear, for on the one side was a government stained by regicide and the excesses of martial law, on the other the white flag of reaction and the advancing insult of foreign conquest.

Napoleon had no difficulty in making his election. Meanly as he thought of Paris politicians he stood for the government of the day,

and in an able dialogue, the *Souper de Beaucaire*, argued against the
Girondins of Marseilles that the cause of the Mountain was the cause
of France. Soon afterwards, on September 16, 1793, at the request
of his Corsican friend Salicetti, he joined the republican army before Toulon as commander of artillery; and it was here that his quality
as a soldier was first decisively shown. He saw, as none had seen
before him, that the problem of the siege was to dislodge the British
fleet from the inner harbour, and that the key to victory was the fort
L'Éguillette on the extreme tip of the western promontory of Caire.
Three months of untiring energy and fearless courage were crowned
with complete success. On December 19, 1793, the troops of the
Convention entered Toulon, and the horrors of the siege were soon
forgotten in the disgrace of reprisals. To the young officer who had
helped procure this brilliant and well-timed victory the government
of Robespierre owed a debt of gratitude. He was promoted to the rank
of brigadier-general, and in the spring of 1794 dispatched at his own
suggestion to Genoa nominally to negotiate for provisions, in reality
to explore the ground with a view to hostilities. But in those days the
life of a republican general, however loyal and eminent, was at the
mercy of any random slander or base intrigue. Bonaparte, as the friend
of the younger Robespierre and the emissary of the Terrorist government, became involved in suspicion after the revolution of
Thermidor. Returning from Genoa with a mind stored with
geographical knowledge, he was accused of being the plan-maker of
the fallen tyrant, deprived of his military rank, and on August 12,
1794, thrown into prison at Fort Carré, near Antibes.

There was nothing compromising in his papers. He had in truth
studiously avoided over-close relations with the dead dictator. When
Maximilien Robespierre offered him a military command in Paris, he
wisely refused it, reckoning that no head could be safe in such a city,
nor could laurels be won there yet. His prudence was rewarded. On
August 20, he was released, and soon afterwards restored to his rank.
How essential were his talents was proved on September 21 at Dego,
when an Austrian force attempting to cut the French communications
with Genoa was routed, largely owing to the skilful dispositions of
the general of artillery.

His heart thenceforward was set upon the Italian command. He
knew the ground and had thought out a plan by which a vigorous
offensive in Italy might shatter the left wing of the continental

coalition. But the Government cried a halt on the Riviera, and then summoned Napoleon to join the Army of the West as an infantry brigadier. Here he would be engaged as an officer in an arm not his own, in a civil war at once desperate and inglorious, against irregular bands of royalist nobles and peasantry. He came to Paris and boldly refused to go, under pretext of illness and reckoning upon the favour of Barras and Fréron, leaders of the dominant party who had seen and duly appreciated his work outside Toulon. For a time success crowned his resolution. He was consulted by the military committee of the Government, and drew up a new plan of campaign in Italy which was accepted and forwarded to the front. Then, by the retirement of Doulcet Pontécoulant, his patron and friend in official quarters, he was left unsheltered. The War Office awoke to his contumacy, and on September 15, 1795, just as he was expecting to be dispatched to Constantinople to organize the artillery of the Sultan, removed his name from the list of generals.

At this crisis of his fortunes Napoleon was saved by the lucky accident of an insurrection in Paris. The Convention, odious on many just accounts not only to the whole royalist connexion, but to all men of moderate opinions, had excited a storm of indignation by decreeing that two-thirds of its members were to sit in the Legislative Assembly established under the new Directoral Constitution. Plain men argued that such a provision exhibited the hollowness of arrangements professedly contrived to conclude the Terror and to give to France an orderly and respectable government. What, they asked, was the use of the new constitution, with its Directory of Five, its Council of Ancients, its Council of Five Hundred, its wise and reassuring precautions against mob rule, if the ship of State was still to be steered by the old gang who had endured the September massacres, killed the King and the Queen, turned Paris into a slaughter-house, and given a recent exhibition of its clemency by doing the Dauphin to death in the Temple prison? The National Guard, some 30,000 strong, determined to wreak vengeance upon the body which had passed the odious 'Law of the Two-Thirds'; and as the Convention had but 5,000 troops under its control, the situation of the Government was gravely imperilled.

From this almost desperate position the Convention was saved on the afternoon of October 5, 1795, by the guns of General Bonaparte. He had obtained an appointment through the friendship and esteem of Barras, who on the previous evening had been placed in command of the Paris troops, and since Barras was no soldier, the brunt of the defence was borne by Napoleon. 'His activity', says Thiébault, 'was astonishing: he seemed to be everywhere at once; he surprised people by his laconic, clear, and prompt orders; everybody was struck by the vigour of his arrangements, and passed from admiration to confidence and from confidence to enthusiasm.' In street-fighting success depends upon artillery, and when Murat galloped in with the guns from the Place des Sablons the victory of the Convention was half secured. As the heads of the insurgents marched from the Church of St. Roch upon the Tuileries they were shot away by a well-directed cannonade; and after a brief struggle, and only at the cost of some 200 lives, the day was won. Had the issue been otherwise, we cannot doubt but that France would have been overwhelmed by a fresh wave of anarchy and civil war. However tarnished its credentials, however discreditable its most recent phase of policy, the Convention was at least as honest in purpose as many of its assailants, and more truly representative of the substantial interests of France. It stood at least for three things, all of which would have been endangered by its overthrow in Vendémiaire: for the revolutionary settlement, for the unity of the nation, and for the defence of the frontiers against foreign arms. Napoleon was rewarded by the command of the Army of the Interior. In saving the Convention he had preserved for France not only a social order grounded on equality, but a regicide government committed to war.

In the first flush of his triumph Bonaparte met and was conquered by a woman. Among the friends of Barras and Tallien was the widow of a certain Marquis Alexandre de Beauharnais, a general in the army of the Republic, who, like many a man as innocent and loyal as himself, had suffered by the guillotine during the dark days of the Terror. Josephine Beauharnais was born in Martinique in 1763, and was gifted with all the subtle charm and seduction of the South. Her voice was low and rich, her features refined, her expression gentle, her lightest movements easy and graceful. Her social tact was as perfect as her figure. Great as were the limitations of her intellect and schooling, she knew how to conceal them, and the most fastidious critics of the Salon found nothing to censure in a creature so distinguished and yet so unconstrained. The young general, whose sallow face, low stature and awkward bearing did not at once commend him to ladies, fell violently in love with this aristocratic widow, six years his senior. That she was poor and the mother of two children did not deter him; and indeed from the worldly point of view (if calculation was mixed with the heat of passion) these advantages were outweighed by her special friendship with the influential Barras. As for Josephine, being of a cooler metal she lost neither heart nor head. But the courage, the confidence, the wide grasp of intellect, the half-terrifying glitter of that searching glance, and the portentous vehemence of that ardent suit subdued her will, and how could she fail to understand that some brilliant destiny was reserved for Napoleon? They were married on March 9, 1796. Two days before, on the motion of Carnot, Napoleon was appointed to the Italian command. The great genius who had organized the victories of the Revolution had discerned the merits of the plan of campaign which had been submitted to the military committee in the summer of the previous year, and wisely decided to entrust General Bonaparte with the task of executing his own design.

2

The Italian Command

THE WAR BETWEEN the French Revolution and the dynasts of
Europe had now run for close upon four years. After an opening
sullied by cowardice, mutiny, and crime, the French armies had
astonished the world by their enterprise and valour. They had
conquered Belgium and Holland, Savoy and Nice, and more than
once raided into Germany, achieving under the tricolour triumphs
consistently pursued but never realized under the white flag of the
Bourbon monarchy. So high was now the measure of French pride
that the recovery of the frontiers of ancient Gaul, which stretched to
the Rhine and the Alps, was a point of diplomatic honour without
which no prospect of peace would receive a moment's consideration.
And this ambition was served not only by the inherited skill and
equipment of the best army in Europe, but by the enthusiasm of a
nation newly born to liberty. The old monarchies, thrifty of mer-
cenary blood, found themselves confronted by a power which was
prepared to spend ten thousand lives a week. Such lavishness was
astounding even to those who remembered the hard blows of
Frederick the Great. The coalition of autocrats, never firmly soldered,
began to dissolve as the difficulties of their enterprise accumulated.
In 1795 Prussia withdrew from the war, carrying with her into the
camp of neutrals all Northern Germany; and her example was
followed by Spain. Russia stood hostile but motionless for her soldiers
were busy in Poland and the life was ebbing from her great Tsarina.
Of the powers which still remained at war with France, Austria
and England were alone important. The continuance of hostilities
on the Continent hinged upon the goodwill of Austria, and since the
Revolution had demoralized the marine service of France, Great

Britain was in a position to capture the French colonies, to waylay the French merchantmen, and to land troops at any point in the French dominions. To obtain from either of these powers a formal acknowledgement of her new claims was clearly for France a task of immense difficulty. The recognition of the doctrine of natural frontiers meant the transference to France of Belgium, with its grand water-way of the Scheldt, which the jealousy of Holland and England had closed to navigation, and its superb port of Antwerp, which under a powerful government might wrest the commercial supremacy from London. Austria would never consent to cede her Belgic provinces to France without compensation, and England was prepared to fight for twenty years rather than see the tricolour wave over Antwerp. But the point of Belgium, justly regarded as vital in London, was not the only matter of contention between Francis II of Austria and the French Republic. As the nephew of Marie Antoinette and the ally of the Bourbon crown, that young, unintelligent, and obstinate prince was concerned to avenge the injuries done to his family and his order. As Holy Roman Emperor he must protect German interests on the Rhine. As the ally of the little kingdom of Sardinia he could not suffer the robbery of Savoy and Nice, for the King of Sardinia was the sentinel posted at the western gate of Italy, and Italy was little better than an Austrian preserve. To exclude the influence of the French Revolution from the peninsula was an Austrian interest even more important than the preservation of Antwerp, the defence of the Rhine, or the avenging of the royal victims of the guillotine.

Napoleon knew that peace with honour was to be won in Italy. In a masterly note submitted to the younger Robespierre, in July 1794, he had advocated a strict defensive on the Spanish and a spirited offensive on the Italian frontier. And now that he was in command of the Army of Italy his plan was to strike up from the Riviera across the Apennines and to cut the connexion between the Sardinian and Austrian armies, who were strung out across the passes north of Savona. Then when each of the opposing armies had been shaken and driven apart on diverging lines, he would push the Austrians out of Italy, and crossing the Tyrol into Bavaria, or striking northwards from the more easterly point of Trieste, join hands with the Army of the Rhine and dictate a peace under the walls of Vienna.

The art of war is closely related to scientific and material progress. In the seventeenth century, when muskets were loaded at the muzzle

and the field artillery was so heavy and unhandy that a dozen guns
was an ample allowance for an army, and half-a-dozen rounds a full
measure for an engagement, battles were won by sword and push of
pike. Such encounters were short and decisive when they occurred,
but they occurred rarely. It took the best part of a day to arrange the
pikemen and musketeers, the cannoneers and the cavalry, in their
elaborate order of battle, and many hours to change the order when
once it had been formed. No prudent general would divide his force
or risk an encounter with an army superior to his own. No army,
however superior, could force an engagement upon an antagonist who
refused to accept one. It was possible for skilful commanders to miss
one another for weeks and to manœuvre without a general action for
the best part of a year.

In the course of the eighteenth century the military art was revolu-
tionized by a series of improvements in firearms. By 1720 the musket
of the foot-soldier was so perfected as to be able to fire more than one
shot a minute. Then came a light serviceable field-gun, then horse
artillery, finally in 1765 the invention by Gribeauval, an officer in the
army of Louis XVI, of a field artillery combining the maximum of
effectiveness with the minimum of weight. The result of all these
changes was not only to give to the artillery arm a new importance
in warfare and to make it for the first time an essential factor in
infantry operations, but to transform the whole science of strategy.
Armies could now break themselves up into divisions, since a division,
given favourable ground, could defend itself against a superior force,
or at least fight its way into safety by a series of rearguard actions;
and so it became the central problem of strategy to consider how this
new power of acting on a wide front with an elastic force could best
be used. By slow and reluctant stages the undivided army and the
stiff old battle array became things of the past. Generals gradually
learnt to throw out detachments and clouds of skirmishers, and to
manœuvre their divisions into action from widely distant points on
the map. The larger the combination, the more necessary an exact
knowledge of roads and gradients. A campaign might be won by map
and compass, a battle decided by the charge of a column upon a force
shaken and demoralized by an effective concentration of artillery
fire.

The principles of strategy adjusted to these changes had been
fully realized and clearly stated by the French military writers of the

ancien régime before any full illustration had been afforded of their practical working. They knew the value of the offensive tactics, of the rapid concentration of divisions before a battle, of the cannonade as a preparation for the charge in column. They saw how horse artillery enabled rearguard actions to be successfully fought. They recommended an extreme mobility only to be purchased by the sacrifice of convoys and by ruthless requisitions from the countryside. The grand principles of military success, that the enemy must be ceaselessly harassed, that he must be manœuvred out of strong positions, that he must be surprised by night marches, and confounded by concentrated attacks upon the weakest part of his line—all this was familiar to every student of Guibert and Gribeauval, of Bourcet and Du Teil. The new strategy was well known to Bonaparte. It is his glory to have applied it and to have exhibited its power.

The French army does not owe to Napoleon any military patents but that of victory. He invented nothing, neither a new gun, nor a new formation, nor new principles of attack and defence. He accepted what he found ready to his hand—the armament, the drill book, the tactics and strategy of the old royal army of France in which he had served his apprenticeship. His tactical preference was for the *ordre mixte*, recommended by Guibert as combining the wide frontal fire of the line with the solid striking force of the column, but this alternation of battalions in line and battalions in column was not invariably adopted, and was often confined to those portions of the field where Napoleon wished to contain the enemy, while at the decisive point the attack was entrusted to great masses of men charging in undeployed column. In the main, however, minor tactical dispositions were left to subordinates. Napoleon's concern was with 'grand tactics', with the movement of divisions on to the field, with the selection of the crucial point to be assailed, and with the concentration of artillery fire upon it. Here he was rarely at fault, but the system of the column, inherited from the armies of the French Revolution, depended for its success upon the unsteadiness of the troops opposed to it. When the opposing army was already demoralized either by the guns or the skirmishing line of its adversary the shock tactics of the column were irresistible: but against a long line of cool and collected marksmen, screened from artillery by the lie of the land, the column was bound to fail. The narrow front of the charging mass was shot away by the converging fire of the extended line, and the battle was lost before the weight of the column could be brought to bear upon its opponent. This is the secret of General Stuart's victory at Maida in 1806 and of Wellington's victories in the Peninsular War; but when Napoleon took over the Italian command in 1796 the superiority of the linear formation was not yet evident, for no army opposed to the French had yet exhibited the perfect steadiness and fire discipline necessary to its success.

The army of France, which in the later days of Louis XVI was already the best in Europe, reached a still higher stage of efficiency as a consequence of the political convulsions of the country. Without loss of scientific precision, for, though many emigrated, the artillerists and engineers of the royal army continued for the most part to serve under the tricolour, it became national and democratic, patient of huge sacrifice, and capable of a degree of mobility new to the practice of war. Free promotion succeeded the stifling system of caste, so that in a few years an able man shot up from the ranks to high command. Human life was held cheap. An army was no longer royal capital to be saved, but national income to be expended. The incredible buoyancy of the nation communicated itself to the camp, and the French soldier of the Republic felt ready to go anywhere and dare anything in the most seductive cause which has ever been placed before a great multitude of men.

When Napoleon took up his Italian command, none of his generals knew him. His extreme youth, his haggard face and mean stature, and the eagerness with which he showed the portrait of his bride, suggested that his appointment was due to favouritism and intrigue. 'But a moment afterwards', says Masséna, 'he put on his general's hat and seemed to have grown two feet. He questioned us on the position of our divisions, on the spirit and effective force of each corps, prescribed the course which we were to follow, announced that he would hold an inspection on the morrow, and on the following day attack the enemy.' Masséna, Berthier, and Augereau were all older men, but the new general spoke with such calm, dignity, and talent that everybody who heard him was convinced that here was a true captain of men. The prodigal energy of the new nation, already fired to a course of heroic adventure, was awaiting just such a leader as this, a man of swift resolve and iron will, a master of the craft of war on its technical side, and yet eloquent, imaginative, studious of popularity, capable in the few words of a proclamation or a bulletin

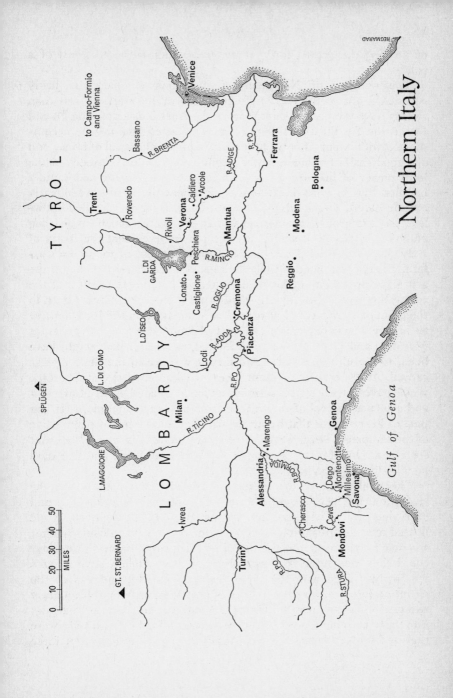

Northern Italy

of striking the great chords of emotion which sway the heart of a
soldier.

The opening of Napoleon's first Italian campaign is justly
accounted one of the classic pieces of the military art. In less than
twenty days the young general drove the Austrians across the Po and
forced the Sardinians to demand an armistice. And this he accomplished with twenty-four light mountain guns, a handful of horse, and
a ragged, half-starving infantry slightly inferior in numbers to the
joint power of his original adversaries, but so skilfully and rapidly
handled that in every important engagement the enemy was greatly
outnumbered. Youth was pitted against age, exact and detailed knowledge of the ground against capacious ignorance; and in explaining
Napoleon's success it should also be remembered that the Army of
Italy was already hardened in the rigorous school of mountain warfare. Yet the prudence of the young general was as remarkable as the
grit and impetuosity of his men. When he had cut the centre of the
enemy's power at Montenotte he did not pursue the Austrians on to
the plain of Lombardy, but turned westwards upon the Piedmontese
to secure his communications with France. He won victories at
Mondovi and Ceva, but was not incited, as a lesser man might have
been, to march upon Turin and dictate a peace in the Piedmontese
capital. At the earliest moment he extorted an armistice at Cherasco
which gave him the strict essentials which he needed—three fortresses
and a secure control of the military roads through Piedmont. It was
part of his strength that he never lost sight of the broad perspective
of the campaign, never wasted time in producing minor and irrelevant
successes. On May 10, he forced the bridge of Lodi, and five days
later rode into Milan.

The vital point of the military operations that ensued was the
strong city of Mantua, which was victualled for four months and
garrisoned by 13,000 Austrian troops. So long as the Black Eagle
floated over the great citadel on the Mincio, the French could neither
advance northwards into the Tyrol nor eastwards upon Trieste, nor
could they rely upon the quiescence of those Italian governments
who sympathized with the old order of the world, and viewed the
irruption into their ancient culture of an atheist and republican army
as a clarion call to anarchy. Four times did the Austrians send armies
into Italy to relieve the beleaguered city, and four times they were
repulsed by Napoleon. And here again the numerically weaker force

was generally so wielded as at the critical point of place and time to outnumber its adversary.

The first army of relief under Wurmser was 50,000 strong. Against it Napoleon had 42,000 men, some 10,000 of whom under Sérurier were besieging Mantua with its garrison of 13,000 Austrians. Upon any rational calculation of chances the army of Wurmser should have won the campaign; but the Austrians made the great mistake of dividing forces, Wurmser marching down the Adige on the eastern side of Lake Garda with 32,000 men, and Quasdanovitch pursuing the western bank with 18,000. Even so the French army of observation was unequal to the task imposed upon it, and at a council of war held at Roverbella on July 30, 1796, it was decided to abandon the siege, to sacrifice the siege train and to throw every available man against the relieving army. Such a resolve, whether first suggested by Augereau or not, was quite in the spirit of French intrepidity and Napoleonic perspective. The abandonment of a siege and the sacrifice of a siege train were losses not to be weighed against the humiliation of a general retirement or the chances of a disaster in the open field. Napoleon's aim was to defeat his enemies in detail before they had time to unite south of the Garda. First Quasdanovitch was repulsed at Lonato on August 3; then two days later Napoleon turned round on Wurmser, who had poured fresh troops into Mantua, beat him in the hotly contested fight of Castiglione, and thrust him back into the Tyrol with a total loss of some sixty guns and 10,000 men. Having thus brilliantly saved a desperate situation, the French commander awaited reinforcements and the news of a victory in southern Germany.

The attack was renewed in September, but with even less of foresight and combination upon the Austrian side. The relieving army under Wurmser again divided itself into two, the one under Davidovitch marching through the Tyrol, the other under the commander-in-chief taking the westerly loop of the Brenta valley. On September 4, Davidovitch with 10,000 men was overpowered at Roveredo by a force exactly double his number under Masséna, Augereau, and Vaubois. Then Napoleon, who had cut into the Brenta valley between the two Austrian commanders, rushed down after Wurmser, and covering fifty-seven miles in sixty hours caught him at Bassano (September 8), dealt him a shattering blow, and sent him reeling into Mantua. The accession of so large an addition to the garrison of a pestilential town was no strengthening of its defences, and at that season of the year Napoleon could afford to count on the co-operation of fever. Without too closely pressing the blockade, for the swamps of Mantua proved as dangerous to besiegers as besieged, he sent entreaty after entreaty to Paris for guns and reinforcements.

The six weeks which intervened between the repulse of the second attempt to relieve Mantua, and the third and most critical struggle of the war, are memorable in the history of the Italian *risorgimento*. The ragged army of the French Republic had been received with enthusiasm by an active and intelligent minority of the citizens of Milan, who, having been indoctrinated with the gospel of liberty, viewed the Catholic religion as effete, the Pope as an impostor, and the Austrian Government as an obsolete tyranny. Napoleon was aware that such sentiments were the property of that limited class who had received a legal, medical, or artistic education, and that the mass of the Italian population was still ignorant and credulous. But coming as he did to Italy as the chief of a republican army, and as the herald of republican ideas, he found it politic to encourage the aspirations of those Italians who desired to taste the fruits of liberty and looked to him to guide them into the land of promise. A wave of democratic enthusiasm passed over Reggio, Modena, Ferrara, and Bologna, and was blessed by the French general. Without waiting for the assent of his masters, he committed his country to the recognition of a Transpadane republic formed out of the territories of these four cities and certain portions of the Papal State. 'It is time', he wrote to the citizens of Reggio, 'that Italy also should be counted among the free and powerful nations.' And to assist the process of emancipation he called for guns and men, and fattened himself, his generals, his army and government on the rich spoils of the country.

With sound military instinct he told the Directory that with the meagre force at his disposal it would be folly to embark upon a war with Rome or Naples. The path of prudence was to make peace with Naples and to amuse the Pope with negotiations until the Austrian storm-cloud had been dispersed. Meanwhile the liberal enthusiasm of the North Italian patriots would be a valuable force enlisted on the French side. And so the Directory, who had enjoined an invasion of South Italy and contemplated a peace with Austria based on the cession of Lombardy in exchange for Belgium, found that the whole political landscape was altered at the fiat of their general. They were pledged to defend republican institutions in Lombardy and Emilia, and to swallow their resentment at the continued rule of a priest and a Bourbon. They learned that not a man could be spared from the north, since an Austrian force 60,000 strong was collecting in the Tyrol and in Trieste for another spring at the blockaders of Mantua.

Indeed, the third act of the Mantuan drama was destined to test to their utmost span the resources of Napoleon's military genius. The new Austrian army was under the supreme command of Alvintzi, a veteran like his predecessors, but in Napoleon's mature judgement the ablest and most obstinate of his opponents; and if the honours eventually rested with Napoleon, it was, on his own confession, because the vigour of youth gave him that slight but decisive advantage in dash and tenacity which turns the balance in an even fight.

As if experience had not sufficiently disclosed the perils of division, the Austrians for a third time advanced upon Mantua in two columns —Alvintzi from his eastern base in Trieste, and Davidovitch from his northern base in the Tyrol. In order to parry this attack it was Napoleon's design himself to march eastwards and beat Alvintzi on the Brenta, and then moving swiftly up the curving river into the Tyrol to place himself on the rear of Davidovitch, whose advance down the Adige was to be arrested by a French corps under Vaubois. No general, however brilliant, can count upon executing his schemes exactly as he conceives them, and the opening of the Arcole campaign was for Napoleon a catalogue of disasters. Neither could Vaubois stop the advance of Davidovitch, nor could Augereau and Masséna force the passage of the Brenta. Early in the morning of October 12, Alvintzi appeared upon the hills of Caldiero outside the walls of Verona. Napoleon marched out to dislodge him, only to find that against such a general posted in a strong position, the famous *élan* of his Army of Italy was unavailing. After a long day's fight the French were repulsed all along the line and driven back into the city. The situation was critical. If Napoleon retreated upon Mantua the two Austrian columns would effect their junction. If he remained in Verona he might be surrounded. If he attempted again to assault the strong position of Caldiero, he would only court a second repulse. With an intuition of genius he determined to march round Alvintzi's position, to capture his transport and reserve artillery, and to fight him before Davidovitch had time to come up, in a position where superior numbers were of little account. So leaving 3,000 men in

Verona he turned his face down the Adige, and crossing, at Ronco on October 15, pushed across the triangle of marshy ground which divides the Adige and the Alpone.

Here an unexpected obstacle confronted the French advance. The bridge over the Alpone at Arcole was held by two Croatian battalions with inflexible tenacity. In vain Napoleon seized a flag, rushed to the bridge, and tried by an example of personal courage to carry the passage. The Austrians poured in a murderous fire from the houses in the little village across the stream, and as man after man fell the general was borne backwards in the retreating tide, thrust sideways from the dyke into the water, and only with difficulty extricated. On the next day the whole of Alvintzi's army was concentrated round Arcole, and a battle began which swayed to and fro until the evening of the 17th. The psychological moment which decides the fate of armies came in the afternoon of the third day, when fifty horsemen led by a negro of the Guides galloped round the rear of the Austrian position, sounding their trumpets and creating the impression of a serious attack. For a moment the ranks wavered, and taking advantage of the sudden recoil, Augereau, who commanded on the French right, pressed home his attack. At five o'clock the army which had so gallantly defended the paltry village of Arcole slowly withdrew from its positions. The victory came not a moment too soon, for on the same day Vaubois was turned out of Rivoli, and the road to Verona was open to Davidovitch. Indeed, had that commander conducted himself with promptitude and resolve, he might have helped to retrieve the defeat of Arcole, for on October 21, the stubborn Alvintzi was back on the heights of Caldiero and in a position to give him support. Fortunately for Napoleon, Davidovitch was not made of the firmest metal, and after being driven from the defensible plateau of Rivoli was soon retreating in disorder before the fierce pursuit of Vaubois and Masséna.

Four months later the all-important question whether Mantua was to be relieved was put to a crowning test on the plateau of Rivoli. Here on January 13, Joubert found himself confronted with a greatly superior army advancing from the north under Alvintzi, and reported that unless speedily reinforced he should be compelled to evacuate the position. At two o'clock on the following morning Napoleon arrived on the ground from Verona. By the sparkling light of a wintry moon he saw the five Austrian camps, their fires starring the country between the Adige and the lake, and from the evidence thus supplied inferred that the battle was timed for ten o'clock, and that for every Frenchman to defend the plateau there would be two Austrians ready to attack it. But the position of Rivoli has this special character, that an army coming from the Tyrol cannot dislodge its defenders save by scaling the spurs which overlook the plateau, and cannot scale the spurs without dispensing with horse and artillery. In the battle which ensued the French, though greatly outnumbered, were supported by sixty guns and several regiments of cavalry against a force compelled to rely on one arm alone. This, coupled with the inspiring activity of Bonaparte and the grand night march of Masséna with reinforcements, decided the day. By 2 p.m. the Austrians were beaten, and had the snow not lain thick upon the pass the pursuit of the flying enemy would not have stopped at Trent. Three weeks later the tricolour was flying over Mantua, and the obstacle which had so long delayed Napoleon's advance was triumphantly removed.

Before that advance was pushed home Napoleon turned aside to settle his accounts with the Pope. Here again he refused to be diverted from the strict essentials of success either by the advice of a cabinet which he despised, or by the prospect of easy victories which could not help to decide the campaign. The Papal Government was unfriendly to the anti-clerical Republic of France, and pressure was put upon General Bonaparte to teach the priests their place in the economy of the republican world. Nothing would have been easier to the tried veterans of the Army of Italy than to proceed in triumph to Rome, and there to annihilate the weakest of governments. Yet the temptation, however alluring, was one which a statesman and a strategist was bound to resist. There was no sense in gratuitously offending the religious susceptibilities of a Catholic people whose goodwill it was important for the French to secure; and so long as Austrian armies were at large, it would be an act of high military imprudence for the general-in-chief of the French army to go to Rome. At the Treaty of Tolentino (February 19) Napoleon wrung tribute, pictures, and provinces from the Pope without compromising his military position. He had delayed his rupture with the Papacy until the fall of Mantua was assured, and so timed his accommodation with the Pope as to be able to strike a fresh Austrian army collecting on the Tagliamento before it was reinforced. The economy of fleeting moments has never been more jealously practised, and that he might gain a few days for his Roman campaign, the task of receiving the submission of Mantua and the sword of the Austrian field-marshal was delegated to Sérurier.

The last phase of the war is characterized by a succession of French victories easily won against an inferior and demoralized enemy. While Joubert pushed his way northwards and eastwards by the Brenner and the Pustherthal, Napoleon beat the Archduke Charles at the Tagliamento, and crossing into Carinthia by the Col de Tarvis steadily drove forward towards the Austrian capital. On March 28 he was at Villach, on April 7 his vanguard under Masséna reached the little town of Leoben, not a hundred miles from Vienna. Here overtures for peace were received and preliminaries signed. With the shrewd judgement which characterized his whole conduct of this campaign, Napoleon knew when it was wise to stop as well as when it was opportune to strike. A further advance would have been dangerous, for apart from the possibility of a grand imperial rally, he had learnt that no help was to be expected from the Army of the Rhine and that peasant risings in Venetia and Tyrol were likely to imperil his communications.

Among the baits offered to Austria in the Preliminaries of Leoben was a share in the ancient and happy Republic of Venice, a state which had sought no quarrel with France and could not properly be described as a tyranny doomed by reason. The responsibility of making the offer rests with Bonaparte, that of accepting it with Thugut, the Austrian Prime Minister. Bonaparte's diplomacy was of his own choosing, and was neither republican nor monarchist. A peace of some kind with Austria he must have, and that soon; and the swiftest way to overcome the reluctance of his enemy to part with Belgium and Lombardy was to offer her Venice in exchange. The ancient fame of this most pleasant haunt of fashionable gamblers was nothing to him; its weakness, so far from carrying an invitation to pity, gave matter for contempt. He could argue with his conscience that he had done enough already for Italian liberty, and that the loss of Venetian freedom was not too heavy a price for Lombard liberty. He had no punctilio as to the procedure. It was easy to pick a quarrel with a government which had not been strong enough to protect its neutrality or to suppress open manifestations of hostility to Jacobin principles. An insurrection at Verona, sternly suppressed by the French garrison, supplied a pretext for demanding a revolution at

Venice. The old government fell cowering to the ground; and with engaging versatility the impressionable Venetians conceived a sudden enthusiasm for the tricolour, the tree of liberty, the red cap, and all the emblems of the French Revolution. It was but a summer's madness. When the first October snows touched the mountain spurs, Napoleon saw that it was time to have the treaty signed, and the Venetians learnt that the tree, the cap, and the tricolour were no sovereign spells against the greatest calamity which can befall a state. The Republic was partitioned, and the hated two-headed eagle waved over the lagoons.

If it is a truism to say that the act was cynical, it would be a shallow philosophy which would summarize Napoleon as a cynic. There is a story of three Venetian envoys secretly dispatched to France to bribe the Directors, but arrested by order of the general-in-chief and hauled back ignominiously to Milan. One of them, a Dandolo, but not of the famous lineage, spoke to his captor with such eloquence that Napoleon was moved to tears, and exhausted all his seductions in trying to prove to the man that the step was a temporary concession to stern necessity. The tears were genuine, and after the battle of Austerlitz the promise was redeemed.

In the history of Italy the most significant feature of Napoleon's political settlement was not the betrayal of Venice, but the foundation of the Cisalpine Republic. Other countries had been betrayed, and in Poland there had been a recent and not more odious precedent of a state annihilated and a nation partitioned by the greed of its neighbours. But the creation of this republic in Northern Italy as the daughter state of France and as the pupil of her Revolution, was at once a challenge to the spirit of national freedom in Italy and an affront to the dynasties whose existence contravened it. Critics might allege that it was a composite and artificial thing made out of Lombardy, the Transpadane, and scraps of Venice and Switzerland, and that being diversely composed it could not endure. It is more important to notice that the boundaries of the new state were so drawn as to comprise the most energetic and progressive populations in Italy, that it was adorned with the established prosperity of Milan, with the learning and patriotic ardour of Bologna, and that unlike the city republics of old whose function and usefulness had been exhausted by the end of the fifteenth century, it was calculated not to enhance but to correct the inveterate curse of Italian localism.

B

Many a family whose members were destined to play an honourable part in the wars of Italian liberation dates the birth of its interest in the national cause to the larger hopes and livelier interests which were kindled by the foundation of the Cisalpine Republic.

It is tempting to suppose that in so framing a seminary for the political education of Italy, Napoleon was obeying the mysterious call of blood. Was he not himself an Italian? Was he not hailed by the Italians as a compatriot? Did he not speak their language and read their hearts? Yet, if there was sentiment on his side, it was no mother of illusion. He saw the faults of the Italian temperament with a merciless lucidity, and argued correctly that a people devoid of strenuous purpose and long unused to the handling of public affairs was not yet ripe for political liberty. His own deep conservative instincts were strengthened by what he saw of the Milanese Jacobin, and though he permitted his new Republic a constitution modelled on the political liberties of France, he named the ministers, the judges, the legislators, and civil servants, and informed the Government in Paris that the Cisalpine Republic was the creation of the army and would crumble to pieces if the army were withdrawn. For the future he trusted that the régime of military conscription would educate the Cisalpines into a due sense of political cohesion and responsibility. Meanwhile the situation was precarious. He knew that the peasantry hated a government which gave them bad paper for their good crops, and he assured the Directors that if once the French bayonets were withdrawn, not a 'patriot' of the new régime would save his skin.

In the spring and summer of 1797, while negotiations were still pending with Austria, and while liberal Italy was being inducted into its new republic, Napoleon kept state in the splendid castle of Mombello, twelve miles from Milan. In all but name he was already a sovereign, giving audience to foreign ambassadors, dining in public, his carriage attended by a Polish bodyguard, his court ruled by a strict etiquette. A shower of Italian odes and sonnets greeted the hero, the peacemaker, the new Hannibal, the protagonist of humanity against despot and caste. Around him was gathered a brilliant assemblage of young officers, full of the exhilarating sense of great exploits already achieved and fresh worlds yet to conquer, unsundered as yet by jealousy and bound in the frank and cordial communion of arms. There, too, was the gay Josephine quieting the suspicions of a passionate bridegroom, and with her were seen the three sisters of the hero, shepherded by their mother, that they might taste the strange sweets of luxury and triumph. Stern and imperious in business hours, Napoleon was all ease and sunshine to his intimates. They admired his pleasant wit, his unaffected gaiety, his rich and brilliant handling of moral and political themes. They found him kindly and not inaccessible to counsel, immensely laborious, but always able to command the precious obedience of sleep. There seemed no limit to the span of his activities and interests. Now he would listen with his staff to Monge discoursing of geometry, now in a lazy interval he would weave dreams and ghost stories. His confidence was boundless, his ascendancy unquestioned: and walking one day in the garden with Miot and Melzi he disclosed something of his ambition. 'Do you think', he asked, 'that I triumph in Italy to make the greatness of the lawyers of the Directory?'

As yet, however, in his own phrase, 'the pear was not ripe'. Much as he despised the Government of France, he was not ready to compass its violent ruin. On the contrary, when in September 1797 it seemed likely that the royalists would capture the machine of state, the revolution was for the second time saved by Napoleon. For three good reasons he could not afford to see the Bourbons back in Paris; they would make peace with Europe, they would govern France, and they would almost certainly dispense with his services. The rule of a corrupt handful of regicides was at least better than the *ancien régime*, for men like Barras could always be bribed and always be put down. So when a cry came from Paris that the elections were reactionary, republican addresses poured in from the Army of Italy, and Augereau, a swashbuckler exactly suited to the task, was dispatched to overawe the capital, and to purify the assemblies of their royalist politicians. The *coup d'état* of Fructidor was brilliantly successful, for it silenced royalism, and established in France a government at once weak, violent, and corrupt. The stars in their courses fought for Bonaparte. In that fatal autumn, Hoche, Pichegru, Moreau, his three most brilliant rivals, fell out of the race, the first dying in early manhood, the other two compromised in the revelations or suspicions of Fructidor. Bonaparte stood higher than ever, his reputation for republican ardour refreshed, the moderate wisdom of his Italian statecraft widely acknowledged. On October 17 he signed the Peace of Campo-Formio with Austria, proving himself more than a match for Cobentzel, than whom there was in Europe no finer or more experienced diplomatist. The proudest monarchy in Europe was compelled to cede Belgium and the Rhine frontier to France, to acknowledge the Cisalpine Republic, and in exchange to accept the shameful guerdon of Venice. The terms were settled by Napoleon, and France and Austria were compelled to swallow them as best they might.

3
Egypt and Syria

OF THE SIX original antagonists of revolutionary France there was
now through the operation of the Peace of Campo-Formio a solitary
survivor. England, the last of the combatants to lay down arms, was
also in the eyes of Napoleon his most formidable opponent, not only
by reason of her wealth, her colonies, and her marine, but also as the
active and irrepressible fomenter of civil discord in France. Austria
had fought stubbornly in the Lombard plains, but no Austrian flag
had fluttered beside the Union Jack in Toulon harbour or in Quiberon
Bay. England, on the other hand, was the principal stronghold of
French royalism, the soul of the continental coalition, and the tyrant
of the seas. With England unsubdued the revolutionary settlement
of France was in constant danger of disturbance. 'Our Government',
wrote Napoleon on October 19, 1797, 'must destroy the English
monarchy, or it must expect itself to be destroyed by these active
islanders. Let us concentrate our energies on the navy and annihilate
England. That done, Europe is at our feet.'

Certainly if England was to be 'destroyed', France could not too
soon attend to her navy. The Revolution, which had given a new mass
and momentum to her armies, had exercised a deplorable influence
on the marine forces of France. A service peculiarly dependent in
almost all its branches upon the possession of technical skill and
experience had been entirely demoralized by the spread of principles
subversive of discipline and impatient of inequality. Serious mutinies
broke out in the dockyards. The trained gunners were disbanded.
Most of the competent officers, belonging as they did to well-born
families, were forced out of the service. The French navy, so efficient
in the American War, lapsed into a state of disorganization from which

it never recovered during Napoleon's ascendancy. And it is one of the fortunate accidents of history that the greatest military tyranny in Europe was so weak upon the seas, that its permanent influence in Asia, Australasia, Africa, and America is summed up in the victory of those forces making for political freedom which were enlisted against it and were secured by its downfall.

It was almost inevitable that the conduct of the war against 'the active islanders' should be entrusted to the young general who had crowned an unparalleled series of victories by a brilliant peace. Napoleon was appointed General of the Army of England. A short inspection of the Channel coast, undertaken in February 1798, showed him that an invasion was impossible without lengthy and meditated preparation. But England was never in Napoleon's eyes a mere island: she was a world power whose principal strength lay in her wide commerce and her Indian possessions. To attack England with success was a feat which could be accomplished in more ways than one. If the Channel was impassable, the Mediterranean was open, and a French army established in Egypt might create just that diversion in the naval forces of his opponent without which it would be folly to attempt the crowning enterprise on London.

The project was recommended by other considerations. From early boyhood Napoleon's imagination had been haunted by the charm, the brilliance, the mystery of the East. To the seafarers of Corsica the Tunisian coast is a familiar and neighbourly region. Tunis leads to Egypt; from Egypt the mind travels through Mecca and Teheran, through Arabian deserts and Persian rose-gardens, to the white temples on the sacred Ganges. As a boy Napoleon had talked of enlisting with the British army in India; as a young general he stood for a few weeks on the brink of a military career in Turkey. In the course of his Italian campaign, as victory after victory confirmed his confidence in destiny, he felt himself drawn more and more power-fully towards the East. He spoke of it frequently to his friends, and began to think of Italy not as an end but as a beginning—a convenient projection so thrown athwart the sea and providentially indented that from its good and numerous harbours it would be easy to master the Mediterranean and the lands which lay beyond. He must have a port looking eastwards, and he seized Ancona; stepping-stones on the Adriatic, and he claimed the Ionian Isles; the control of Genoa, and he created a Ligurian Republic. With the eye of faith he saw Greece fired to revolution by his agents, and the Turkish Empire pushed by a few adroit and skilful strokes down its road to inevitable dissolution. The seizure of Egypt, should it be successfully accomplished, might change the political weights and balances of the world. One possibility was that while an English fleet was kept hovering round Alexandria, Napoleon might return to the Channel, surprise a passage, and overthrow the British Government. A less decisive but not less attractive issue to the enterprise was that after Egypt had been conquered and a Suez Canal pierced and fortified, a French force should march upon India, and joining hands with the Mahrattas expel the English from their Eastern dominions. Or if both these projects should prove impracticable, it would still be an attractive occupation for the master of Egypt to invade Syria, to take Constantinople, and to break the Ottoman Empire to pieces.

For Napoleon at least it was a part of prudence to escape with as little delay as possible from the critical atmosphere of Paris. Being less than forty years of age, he was ineligible for a place in the Directory, and he was acutely conscious of the palsy which spreads over the most brilliant reputation if it is not refreshed by action and advertisement. 'Bourrienne,' he said to his secretary on January 29, 1798, 'I do not wish to remain here; there is nothing to do. They will not listen to anything. Everything wears out here. My glory is already threadbare. This little Europe is too small a field. Great celebrity can be won only in the East.' The example of Alexander was before his eyes. He imagined that beyond Europe, with its stiff traditions and stifling atmosphere of civilized prudence, there were vast and plastic spaces in the world—scenes of 'great empires and great cataclysms' which he might conquer and mould to his will.

The Directors readily accepted the scheme. Ever since the crusade of St. Louis, France had looked upon Egypt as being of all parts of the nearer East that which was most specially designed for her consumption. Its civilization was old, famous, and decayed, its military power reported to be inconsiderable, its Government lodged in the hands of the alien and tyrannous Mamelukes. The conquest of the Nile valley by France had been recommended by Leibnitz, the most famous of German philosophers, and projected by Choiseul, the one efficient adviser of Louis XV. It would undoubtedly annoy the English, and it would temporarily remove from the sphere of domestic politics a man who was already too great for a subject and too dangerous for a democracy. The chief difficulty, that of finance, was overcome in a manner characteristic of republican France. Switzerland was invaded on a flimsy pretext, and out of the lucrative spoiling of Berne, three million francs were allotted to the conquest of Egypt.

On May 19, 1798, Napoleon set sail from Toulon, attended by a brilliant galaxy of generals, savants, artists, and engineers, and leading an army of 38,000 seasoned and proven troops. Berthier was again chief of the staff; Marmont, Lannes, Murat, Desaix, Kléber were among the generals; a corps of illustrious mathematicians, geologists, antiquarians, and chemists advertised the civil preoccupations of the general-in-chief. This was to be no vulgar conquest. Napoleon, who had been recently elected a member of the Institute, was fired with the idea of bringing the dark and mysterious land of the Pharaohs into the full light of scientific knowledge. He would understand the East, its laws and customs, its art and archaeology, its industry and agriculture, above all its religion, which is the warp and woof of Oriental life. The Bible and the Koran should be part of his political library. He would cajole the East in its own language and through the medium of its own ideas. Through him France should become an Egyptian power, intelligent, sympathetic, stooping to the mind and developing the resources of the country, and above all drawing from its inert and plentiful population fresh supplies of military strength.

The convoy of 400 slow-moving transports from France to Egypt was attended by enormous and imponderable risks. With Nelson in the Mediterranean, and everything depending on rapidity, Napoleon had the temerity to attack Malta, and the good fortune to find that an almost impregnable fortress was held by a garrison of traitors and cowards. Valletta was surrendered on June 13, and the French flotilla arrived off Alexandria on July 1. The disembarkation was uncontested, but had Napoleon arrived three days earlier, he would have found Nelson and thirteen 74s waiting to give him a reception. While the English Admiral was racing for Egypt, Napoleon had astutely directed his fleet to skirt the southern shore of Candia (Crete). With a little less loitering on the one side and a little more patience on the other, the greatest soldier and the greatest sailor in history would have met in a naval battle which could have ended only in a crushing disaster for the French.

To attack Egypt with success it is necessary to march upon Cairo, pursuing either the extreme eastern or the extreme western channel of the Nile, and above all avoiding the Delta triangle, with its intricate web of marsh and canal which proved so fatal to the crusade of St. Louis. Napoleon intuitively perceived the essential conditions of Egyptian strategy. Advancing from Alexandria along the western route, he opposed to the impetuous cavalry of the Mamelukes an army ranged in squares and powerfully assisted by artillery. A crushing victory near the Pyramids, obtained at a trifling cost and only twenty-three days after the landing, gave him Cairo and the mastery of Lower Egypt. Had the Nile been high, the pursuit would have been carried further, and the broken fragments of the Mameluke hosts would never have had time to reform.

Decisive as were the initial successes of 'the father of fire', the position of the French army in the midst of a fanatical Moslem population was necessarily insecure. Napoleon was alive to the necessity of humouring the religious prejudices of a superstitious race. He remembered how Alexander the Great, visiting the Temple of Ammon, had caused himself to be declared the Son of Jupiter, 'doing more by that act to assure his conquests than if he had summoned a hundred and twenty thousand Macedonians to his aid'. He would tread the same path of wise accommodation. In the famous school of Gama-el-Azbar at Cairo, sixty doctors, or *ulemas*, were wont to deliberate on points of law and to explain the sacred books. To these solemn guardians of Moslem orthodoxy the anxious theologian from Corsica would gravely expose the state of his devout and trembling soul, would propound questions of Holy Writ, and express his extreme veneration for the Prophet. It was represented to the Arab teachers that but for two obstacles, wine and circumcision, the first proscribed and the second enjoined by the express text of the Koran, there was good ground for expecting a general conversion of the French in Egypt. And since the acute atheism of the Republican Army was as yet luckily unaffected by Catholic practice, it was indicated that the precious seed would fall upon a virgin soil. That nothing might be wanting to complete the delusion, designs were drawn by order of Napoleon for the construction of a mosque large enough to contain the whole French army on that blessed and not too distant day when, by the operation of grace, it should be brought to acknowledge that there is no God but Allah, and that Mohammed is His prophet.

The work of Napoleon in Egypt was rudely disturbed by two

events, each of which might have been surmised as not unlikely to occur—a British victory at sea and a breach of friendship between France and Turkey. On August 1 the French fleet was destroyed by Nelson in Aboukir Bay, and the communications of the army with France abruptly and effectually severed. The news of a reverse far less crucial than this has often sufficed to demoralize an army. Napoleon's troops were already bitterly disappointed with Egypt. They expected palaces of marble and they found hovels of mud; wine, and they were put off with brackish water; welcome, and at any moment, if straying from camp, they were liable to murder and mutilation. To men in such a temper any fresh aggravation might have been the signal for mutiny. But when the news of the disaster reached Cairo Napoleon received it with composure. Summoning his officers around him he addressed them with superb and unruffled confidence. He touched upon the vast resources of Egypt awaiting development, and observed that a country which had once been a powerful monarchy might in the advanced state of science and industry not only return to its former prosperity, but advance to an inconceivable pitch of greatness. He reminded them that their position was impregnable, encamped as they were in a land with no frontiers but the desert on one side and a flat, unsheltered coast on the other. Above all things he exhorted them to preserve the army from discouragement, and to remember that occasions such as these were the crucible of character. 'We must raise our heads', he added in a proud and imaginative conclusion, 'above the floods of the tempest and the floods will be tamed. We are perhaps destined to change the face of the East, and to place our names by the side of those whom ancient and medieval history recalls with most brilliance to our memory.'

A month later Turkey declared war on France, and Napoleon's position in Egypt became exposed to new dangers from within and without. Firmans from the Sultan were read aloud in the mosques, calling upon the Faithful to eject the enemy of Islam, and a portion of the Cairene population acting upon this advice was punished with Oriental severity for its dangerous rebellion. In the following January while Napoleon was at Suez, examining the traces of the old canal which connected the Nile with the Red Sea, he learnt that Ahmed Pasha (surnamed Djezzar the Slaughterer), the Grand Vizier and Governor of Syria, had collected an army for the invasion of Egypt, and that El Arish, the frontier fortress, had fallen into the hands of his vanguard. No intelligence could have been more welcome to Napoleon than a move which gave to the invasion of Syria the character of a defensive operation. He felt that it was time to refresh the confidence of his troops by new triumphs. He could not return to France as he originally intended, nor without considerable reinforcements march upon India; but the conquest of Syria presented a combination of advantages. It would undoubtedly be easy, it would secure the eastern frontier of Egypt, deprive England of a naval base, spread the fame of Napoleon far and wide through the East, and supply a convenient point of departure for the conquest of Asia Minor and European Turkey. For a third time Bonaparte would assume the role of a deliverer. As he had delivered Italy from the Austrians and Egypt from the Mamelukes, so he would now proceed to rescue the suffering population of Syria from the intolerable yoke of Djezzar.

The Syrian campaign, conducted under parching skies and to the accompaniment of thirst, hunger, and plague, ended before the walls of a trumpery seaport town in the repulse which changed the destinies of the world. At first the small army of Bonaparte carried all before it. It took El Arish, stormed Jaffa, and then (March 19, 1799) sat down to besiege Acre, the residence of the slaughtering Vizier. Here a demonstration was made of the truth that a country possessing a seaboard can never be wholly conquered, if the defending force is strong and the attacking force impotent on the water. The enemy who foiled Napoleon at Acre was not the blundering and murderous Turk, but the sea-power of England adroitly used by that vain, eccentric, and chivalrous hero, Sir Sidney Smith. The English admiral, helped by the admirable science of Picard de Phélippeaux, a French royalist engineer, threw such vigour into the defences that for more than two months this inconsiderable fortress resisted the mines, bombardments, and assaults of Napoleon. On May 20 the siege was raised. Plague had broken out in the French camp, ammunition had run short, and the casualties in the two crowning assaults were not far short of 3,000. Intelligence of a Turkish fleet heading for the Delta showed Napoleon that not a moment must be lost. On June 14, after a march of more than 300 miles on short rations and over broken tracks, the army of Syria was back in Cario, having shown in this wonderful race of twenty-six days what hardships men may endure and what feats they may be driven to perform by the iron will of a great commander.

Despite the wastage of war and plague, Napoleon had a force in Egypt sufficient, if cleverly disposed, to deal with the immediate danger from the north. The Turks, 15,000 strong, landed at Aboukir and then waited behind indifferent entrenchments until Napoleon was ready for the assault. If the comparative percentage of casualties is the crucial measure of success in a battle, the French victory won on July 25 was the most complete in history. The Ottoman army, attacked by a force of little more than half its numbers, but infinitely its superior in leadership, dash, and equipment, was shot down, driven into the sea, and destroyed to a man. Every circumstance connected with Napoleon's conduct of the operations was marked by sovereign qualities of precision, rapidity, and resolve—the evacuation of Upper Egypt, the quick concentration of the striking force, the solidity of the attack on the central earthworks, the brilliant charge, delivered at the psychological moment, of Murat's cavalry on the left wing. The reverse of Acre was obliterated by the triumph of Aboukir.

More than two months before the battle Napoleon had resolved to escape from Egypt. In March, while encamped before the walls of Acre, he received intelligence from home that war had again broken out on the Continent, and that Russia, Austria, Sardinia, and Naples were in league against the Republic. He then told General Dommartin that he intended to return to France with a few of his generals. The arguments for the adoption of such a course, plausible in March, were strengthened by news received through the malice of an enemy. Sir Sidney Smith, cruising off Alexandria, supplied Napoleon with a packet of newspapers from which he learnt that the French had been swept out of Italy, and that the soil of France was once more exposed to the risk of invasion. In these circumstances even the purest patriot, assuming that he was conscious of transcendent military ability, might have argued that his place was home and his task the defence of his country. Napoleon, from motives certainly not unmixed with personal ambition, came to the same conclusion. Loudly professing indignation at the corrupt and ignorant Government which had squandered the triumphs of Arcole and Rivoli, he divined with secret pleasure that the incompetence of the Directors was his own opportunity. Very secretly, therefore, on the night of

August 21, he set sail from Alexandria, accompanied by Monge and Berthollet and the seven ablest officers in his command. The splendid soldiers who for his sake, under strange and tropical skies, had faced hunger and thirst, wounds and death, suddenly found themselves deserted by their chief; and even Kléber, the capable general to whom the command was bequeathed, first learnt of his appointment by letter when it was too late to protest by word of mouth.

So the Egyptian romance, which had begun in a blaze of glory, ended in a conspirator's flight. On any sound estimate of probabilities the enterprise was bound to fail, partly by reason of the English supremacy at sea, and partly because no conquest of Egypt can ever be secure until the wild Arabs of the Sudan have been thoroughly subdued. But even admitting that it had been possible for the genius of Napoleon so to rivet the French dominion on the Nile valley that it could defy a maritime blockade and the long attrition of a desert war, the two larger designs to which Egypt was to serve as a modest prelude were wildly impracticable. When we consider the hardships which the small French expeditionary force endured in its comparatively short march through Syria, the difficulties of the commissariat, the wastage through disease, and the losses in battle, how could the Indian expedition, undertaken with a force larger and therefore more difficult to support, and travelling over greater distances and through countries far more barren and far less explored than Palestine, have ended otherwise than in disaster? Nor was the plan of overturning the Turkish Empire, which was unfolded to Bourrienne just before the raising of the siege of Acre, much more promising. An army of 9,000 men marching in the height of summer from Acre to Constantinople would not arrive at its destination intact. Assuming that Napoleon succeeded in bringing 7,000 men to the shores of the Bosphorus, how would he cross? and how would he take Constantinople, defended as it was sure to be by the united strength of the British and Turkish navies? Both schemes were touched with insanity, and if the conquest of Constantinople was a serious project only relinquished through the resistance of Acre, then Sir Sidney Smith stood between Napoleon and failure.

But the fact that there was an element of unsound calculation in the whole Egyptian expedition, and more particularly in the two unrealized projects which were embroidered upon it, does not disparage the grandeur and permanence of its results. Napoleon

introduced Egypt to the methods of a civilized government, and
Europe to the scientific study of the ancient monuments and language of the Nile valley. 'For the first time since the Roman Empire,'
he writes when recounting the expedition of Desaix to Upper Egypt,
'a civilized nation, cultivating the arts and sciences, was about to
visit, measure, and explore those ruins which for so many centuries
have engaged the curiosity of the learned world.' A trilingual inscrip-
tion discovered at Rosetta by a French officer in Napoleon's army
put into the hands of Champollion the key to the hieroglyphs; and *The
Description of Egypt*, a monumental work built out of the observations
and researches of the savants who accompanied the army, is the first
scientific and comprehensive account of the country which 400 years
before Christ inspired Herodotus to write the most famous and
brilliant pages of his history.

Upon Napoleon himself the Egyptian and Syrian campaigns shed
a new and romantic lustre. Genius could ask for no better advertisement than the rapid conquest, however superficial, of two lands bound
up with all the oldest and most hallowed memories of the Christian
polity. Alexandria, the Pyramids, Jaffa, Nazareth, what names were
more familiar than these—so famous in sacred and profane antiquity,
and now illustrated anew by the victories of Bonaparte! The bulletins
from the seat of war gave no indication of failure, for even the repulse
at Acre was disguised as a triumph. Rather they imparted to their
French readers a thrill of pride in the wonderful youth whose brilliant
course among the classic scenes of the ancient world exceeded the
French epic of the Crusades, and shone out in dazzling contrast
against the gloomy and sordid canvas of domestic disorders and
defeats.

4

The Organization of France

Months before a voter was invited to the polls, France had by a *plébiscite* of the heart entrusted its destinies to Napoleon. When he landed at Fréjus after the long obscuration of a six weeks' voyage, a thrill of delirious joy shot through the country, as though at last a sovereign medicine were found for all the diseases of the body politic. The government of lawyers had fallen into the last stage of discredit. The country was tired of war and revolution. It was reasonable to assume that the conqueror of Italy and the organizer of Egypt, a man standing apart from the violent feuds and trivial commotions of Paris, and uncommitted to any cause save that of the Republic, would discover some means of ending a situation daily becoming more intolerable; that he would force the Austrians, Russians, and English to an honourable peace; that he would still the royalist trouble in the Vendée; that he would put down the socialists and the brigands, mend the roads, restore the finances, and give to France the inestimable boon of a just, fair, and regular government. So in medieval Italy a town rent by furious discord would invite the impartial award of an alien judge.

It is this state of the public mind first declared in the tumultuous welcome of October, and afterwards expressed in legal form through the *plébiscite*, which gives to Napoleon's Government its apology and foundation. Unlike the monarchs of Berlin, Vienna, or St. Petersburg, Napoleon drew his power not from descent but from the fountain of popular will. He claimed that he was the child of the Revolution, that the voice of millions favoured his rise and sanctioned his dominion. And this conception of a government neither republican nor monarchical, but partaking of both qualities, each in an extreme form, inasmuch as it was both absolute in power and popular in origin, is part of his political bequest to France. Against authority so derived, governments depending on heredity or set up by foreign armies necessarily appeared illegitimate and the formal logic of democracy was on the side of the Bonapartists, who, after the Bourbons had been placed on the French throne as the result of an English victory, declared that aliens could neither make nor unmake lawful governments in France, and that a nation could alone rightfully abolish the authority which a nation had solemnly conferred.

The method by which Bonaparte made himself master of France is characteristic of the man and the age. He overturned the constitution by ruse and violence: 'It is the epoch of my life', he explained to Mme de Rémusat, 'in which I have shown most ability.' On his arrival in Paris, with the laurels of Aboukir freshly glistening on his brow, and all France acclaiming him as a hero, he suddenly put off the soldier and appeared in the role of the modest and studious civilian. Now he would read a paper to the Institute on Egyptian archaeology, now he would stroll out into the streets in the company of an illustrious savant. *Cedant arma togae*. It was his design to advertise himself not as the brilliant gambler in empires, but in his other aspect, as a man versed in the arts of peace, eager for knowledge and respectful of intellect. For many weeks he contented himself with observing the political eddies of the town, exploring every party but committing himself to none. Then, finding that there was within the Directory a man of like purpose to himself, he entered into confederacy with the Abbé Siéyès and plotted the *coup d'état* of Brumaire.

Even a discredited constitution cannot safely be exploded into the air without a nice attention to detail. The two conspirators, the one a man of action who believed in the autocracy of the sword, the other a philosopher who had framed a scheme of checks and balances, were only so far agreed that both wished to destroy the Directory with as little offence as possible to the Republican conscience of the country. But herein exactly lay the difficulty of the problem. Republicanism was still the strongest political power in France; it was the creed of generals like Jourdan and Moreau, of two out of the five Directors, of the great majority of the Council of Five Hundred. No revolution could be successful which appeared to put in question the issue which for the vast majority of active political minds in France was once and for all decided by the abolition of the monarchy. It was, therefore, necessary to tread delicately. Since Bonaparte could not by reason of his youth be brought into the Directory, it was decided that the Directors should simultaneously resign, and that upon the news of this event the two Legislative Councils should entrust the revision of the constitution to the architects of the plot.

The design was simple and bold, but demanded a campaign of anxious intrigue crowned by a sudden demonstration of force. Active exploration showed that three of the Directors were not to be counted on, that sixty of the Ancients were doubtful, that nothing could be hoped from the Five Hundred, and that the temper of the Jacobin workmen made Paris a dangerous scene for an anti-Jacobin experiment. Accordingly it was arranged that the Council of Ancients should take advantage of its constitutional right to decree the transfer of the Legislature to Saint-Cloud on the pretext of a conspiracy dangerous to its deliberations. There, at a safe distance from the fiery humours of the Paris workshops, and in the midst of a park filled with his war-soiled and obedient veterans, Bonaparte might extract from the last revolutionary Assembly of France its official death-warrant. The plan was duly executed on 18 and 19 Brumaire (November 9 and 10, 1799), days memorable in history as witnessing the rise of Napoleon to civil power. When the Ancients had passed their decree on the morning of the 18th, Napoleon rode down to the Tuileries at the head of a brilliant cavalcade and swore an oath to preserve a free and equal Republic. Afterwards, to the secretary of a Director who came to meet him in the gardens, he spoke words which resounded through the length and breadth of the country: 'What have you done with this France which I left so brilliant! I left you peace, I find war. I left you victories, I find defeat. I left you the millions of Italy, I find laws of spoliation and misery.' But on the next day his adjurations fell with less effect on the angry and suspicious legislators who were gathered together in the palace of Saint-Cloud. They saw themselves trapped into the midst of a hostile army upon the pretext of a plot which they suspected to be imaginary, and in the interests of a scheme which they divined to be little else than rule of the sword. When, after a wild and incoherent speech to the Ancients, Bonaparte suddenly appeared in the Orangery, where the Lower House, presided over by Lucien, was holding its session, a sudden storm of passion surged up against him and he was borne fainting from the hall. Then it was that the clever but shallow rhetorician, who by a fortunate accident was in the chair, for the second time influenced the life of Napoleon. While the members were howling for a decree of outlawry, Lucien slipped away, rode out to his brother in the park, and called upon the troops to deliver the Assembly from a pack of audacious brigands, the hirelings of Pitt who were destroying its liberties. The melodrama was congenial and the lie effective. A few minutes later in that dim November afternoon the bayonets of the grenadiers gleamed in the entrance of the Orangery, and a huddled band of red-robed deputies rushed for the doors, leapt out of the windows, and swiftly scattering through the gloom of the trees and bushes were lost to view and to history. In the early dawn a small committee of both Chambers, selected from the partisans of revision, decreed a provisional government consisting of Bonaparte, Siéyès, and Roger Ducos pending the elaboration of organic laws. So without a drop of blood shed and to the measureless satisfaction of the country the long reign of the Jacobins was brought to an end.

The constitution which was set up a month later, while preserving the show of political liberty, placed the supreme power in the hands of Bonaparte. In deference to the current practice of regarding Rome as the parent of republican virtue, the highest executive officers were styled Consuls, and the apparatus of government was supplied with a Tribunate to debate the bills and a Senate to safeguard the Constitution. But no astute person was deceived by these analogies, nor by the contrivances, due to the ingenuity of Siéyès, for gradually filtering the currents of public opinion into the central cisterns of government. The First Consul during the ten years of his office was to be master of the State. He named the ministers, controlled the administration, and called the policy. The real legislative organ was neither the Tribunate, which could speak but not vote, nor yet the Legislature, which could vote but not speak; but the Council of State, a body of chosen experts to whom was entrusted under the presidency of the First Consul the duty of drafting and initiating laws. Neither was a check upon autocracy supplied by the plural character of the supreme executive committee. Napoleon's colleagues were neither rivals of his power nor critics of his policy. The one, Cambacérès, an able jurist, drawn from the ranks of the Jacobin regicides, expended such time as he could spare from the law upon the delights of the table; the other, Lebrun, was simply a modest and cultured savant of the old monarchy, caught up and tied to the

triumphal car of Napoleon as a signal pledge that even such ante-
cedents were no bar to service under the new régime.

In place of the old revolutionary watchwords, the mottoes of the
new Government were splendour, comprehension, and efficiency.
Democracy has been rich in statesmen who have known how to
appeal with varying degrees of refinement to the imagination of great
masses of men; but in the art of decorating government for the public
eye Napoleon is pioneer and prince. The vision of ancient Rome,
shining in the trophies of its worldwide conquest and covering half
Europe with its causeways and baths, its marble amphitheatres and
gigantic aqueducts, was continually before him; and what Rome had
done and been in the past, Paris might do and be in the present. He
conceived it as belonging to the province of statesmanship not only
to make laws and to administer provinces, but to bequeath to posterity
visible memorials of its grandeur. The idea of making Paris the capital
of European art and scholarship had been entertained by the Directory, and was promoted by the spoliations of Napoleon's first
campaign in Italy. Now that he was master of France the flowing tide
of foreign conquest might again contribute to swell domestic magni-
ficence; and to this design was superadded the project of giving the
world a new conception of the degree to which the public works and
industrial arts of a country could be promoted by an active and
splendour-loving Government.

It was a second article in Napoleon's creed that government should
be founded on a broad base. Soldiers who learn their politics in the
stern school of war are not hampered in their choice of instruments
by a nice regard for variances in theology or politics. Napoleon chose
his servants, as Cromwell his soldiers, upon a wide principle of
toleration. He meant Jacobins, Girondins, and Royalists to receive
the shelter of equal laws, and in the discipline of his employment to
outgrow the narrowing embitterment of the recent strife. The laws
against the *émigrés* were relaxed; the Catholic Church was soon made
to feel that the era of persecution was over, and that the new Government was disposed to come to an accommodation with the religious
conscience of the country. 'When my service is in question,' said the
First Consul, 'all passions must be laid aside.'

Of efficiency in administration there has been no greater master,
for this depends not only on industry and methods, on grasp of
principle and attention to detail, but also on the rarer powers of

inspiration and command. Napoleon could at a pinch work eighteen hours in the twenty-four. 'He would often', says Chaptal, 'keep his Councils for eight or ten hours, and it was always he who bore the burden of the talk and contention.' At any hour of night or morning, after any spell of exhausting work, nobody saw his mind otherwise than keen and alert. His cross-examination of experts was quick, searching, and thorough, his tenacity such that he never attacked a subject without pursuing it to the point at which certainty emerged. Being sober in his habits, with no predilection for any particular food, and rarely spending more than ten or twelve minutes at table unless the conversation pleased him, he was a miracle and pattern of labour to his subordinates. Without any systematic education, with little Latin and no Greek, constantly mispronouncing French words, saying *section* for *session*, *fulminant* for *culminant*, *voyagères* for *viagères*, he nevertheless in a few months established an intellectual ascendancy over the strongest and best-trained minds in Paris. His confidence in his own powers—a great point in a man—was boundless. On occasions when his councillors differed from him, he would tap his head saying, 'This good instrument is more useful to me than the advice of men who are accounted well-trained and experienced,' and so he went his own way, trusting to his intuition, to his exact and capacious memory, to his exquisite lucidity of mind, snatching, as he went with savage rapidity, the scraps of intellectual food which were auxiliary to action. In finance and account-keeping he was the most rigorous and exacting of masters, and every clerk who drove a quill in a government office knew at once that the day of the sloven was over, and worked with treble energy as if the stern eye of Napoleon were glaring down upon his desk. In all the mechanical side of administration, down to the rules for a card-index or catalogue, he had nothing to learn from subordinates. And in the spirit of direction, which is more important than any mechanism, he was unequalled. In civil, as in military, affairs the dispatches of the First Consul receive no injury from the impetuous haste with which they were dictated to his secretaries. They are terse and peremptory, but never fumbling and obscure, and so expressive of the native temperament of their author, that the reader who opens a volume no matter at what place seems to hear the hard, imperious utterance and to take heat from the movement of the glowing mind.

It was probably essential to the restoration of efficient government in France that the will of Napoleon should be unobstructed by local liberties. A system of local government can hardly work well without some kind of aristocracy, or at least some general measure of mutual confidence. Neither of these conditions was present in 1799. The French Revolution had destroyed the old aristocracy of France and scattered the seeds of hate and faction broadcast through the land. Napoleon, therefore, was driven by circumstances to revert to the centralization whch had been the cardinal feature of French government ever since the days of Richelieu. The prefect in the department, the sub-prefect in the arrondissement, the mayor in the commune are the creatures of the central government and the obedient instruments of its will. This, in a word, is tyranny; but perhaps no medicine less drastic could have cooled the poisonous fevers which for the last ten years had been raging in the body politic of France.

There was to be no return to the *ancien régime*. It was not the least among the many benefits conferred by Napoleon that the bad forms of social privilege, abolished by the first revolutionary assembly, found no place in his system, and that the peasant under his powerful rule acquired a fresh sense of certainty that never again would he be plagued by the game laws, the courts, and the exactions of the seigneur. The Legion of Honour, a non-hereditary decoration conferred for military and civil services, was attacked by the purists of equality but defended by Napoleon as a spur to ambition and an instrument of government. 'It is with baubles', he said, 'that men are led.' Nor was there any material change in the law of inheritance as it was left by the revolutionary assemblies. The civil code proceeds upon the idea that in the main it is a desirable thing that properties should be equally divided at death, though a certain proportion of the inheritance (*quotité disponible*) may be bequeathed at the discretion of the testator. In the bad old days of the monarchy industry and commerce were throttled by guild regulations, internal customs dues, and a fiscal system so iniquitously calculated that its principal weight fell on those who were least able to bear it. These inequalities, rudely and suddenly swept away in the storm of the Revolution, were never allowed to reappear. Napoleon knew that however small a price France might set upon political liberty, she would never tolerate the restoration of social privilege. He offered 'a career open to talent', holding it to be at once the criterion of democracy and one of the prime secrets of statesmanship, so to provide that no citizen, however humble, should be debarred by disparagement of birth and connexions from the highest office and eminence in the State.

If any further proof is wanted of the continuing influence of the Revolution, it is provided by the fact that Napoleon adopted and confirmed the revolutionary land-settlement. In the question which of all other questions touched most deeply the material interests of the country he sided not with the reaction but with the Revolution. He never proposed to ask the peasant to disgorge the acres of the priest and the noble, which during the ten years of pandemonium had passed, sometimes by purchase at a derisory rate, sometimes even without that formality, into his hands. On the contrary, it was an essential part of Napoleon's policy to fortify these ambiguous and disputed titles, and to secure for them not only the protection of the State but even the sanction of the despoiled and outraged Church. No course could have been more prudent than so to enlist upon the side of the new Government the greatest and most characteristic economic interest in France. Every peasant recognized in Napoleon his protector; and as the religious reformation in England was made secure by the distribution among the squirearchy of the rich plunder of the Catholic Church, so the protection accorded by the First Consul to the new titles acquired during the Revolution was the most effective pledge which could be given to the nation that the old order would never be restored.

There was the more reason for insisting upon these essentials of the new democracy, since in other parts of his policy Napoleon was determined to discard the practice of the later Revolution. In no department of his work did he encounter a greater mass of criticism, whispered or unavowed, than in his dealings with the Church. It had become a fashion, not only with the learned class, but with that great body of active *bourgeoisie* who controlled the course of the Revolution, to dismiss religion as a foolish lie and to see in the Church an organ of obscurantism, privilege, and oppression, whose power should be abridged and whose activities should be jealously surveyed. Probably the whole cultivated society of Paris, most of the generals and officers of the army, and a large proportion of the more successful politicians, were now declared infidels or indifferents. They viewed the priest as the prey of a decaying superstition, as the ally of the foreigner and the enemy of his country. And to this conviction expression had been fully given by the law-givers and administrators of the Revolution.

In 1791 the Constituent Assembly despoiled the Church of its landed property, placed it upon a reduced establishment, and asked it to accept a democratic constitution, possibly countenanced by the practice of the Apostolic Age, but certainly repugnant to the custom of recent centuries and to the Catholic conscience. All over the country honest and scrupulous Catholics refused to take the oath of the new Constitution. They were persecuted with every device the ingenuity and intolerance of that age could suggest, but intolerance has often failed before and it failed then. The schism in the Church persisted, the refractory clergy celebrating before crowds in the fields and woods, the 'constitutionals' enjoying the barren splendour of empty cathedrals. Eventually even the meagre salaries of the faithful 'constitutionals' became too great a burden for the bankrupt Treasury. The Catholic Church was disestablished. The State declared its neutrality in the sphere of religious dogma. But lest the revolutionary settlement should be imperilled by the manifestation of beliefs, safe only when secluded, no priest might go in procession, fluttering the white surplice in the streets, nor church bell ring into the air its simple summons to devotion.

While preserving the agnosticism of his early manhood, Napoleon did not share the view that religion was a decaying power in the world. He knew the story of the Vendée and had seen the Italian peasant at his shrine. All through the Catholic world he descried in the country-folk a simple faith in saints and miracles, in the godly rule of the Holy Father of Rome, in the efficacious intercession of the Mother of Christ in heaven. To the statesman such spiritual forces swaying the lives of the agricultural and military class were all-important. He must annex and control them. Religion was not to be dismissed like a discarded theory in chemistry. It was 'the mystery of the social order', the 'vaccine' against grosser forms of charlatanism, the golden hope which kept the outcasts of the world in bondage to a lot otherwise intolerable.

One evening as he strolled with a councillor of state in the park of Malmaison, Bonaparte opened a conversation on religion. 'I was here last Sunday,' he said, 'walking in this solitude, this silence of Nature. The sound of the church bell of Ruel suddenly struck upon my ear. I was moved; so strong is the power of early habit and education. I said to myself, "What an impression that must make upon the simple and credulous." How can your philosophers and ideologues answer

that? The people must have a religion, and that religion must be in
the hands of the Government. . . . People will say that I am a Papist.
I am nothing. I was a Mahommedan in Egypt, I shall be a Catholic
here for the good of the people. I do not believe in religions . . . but
the idea of a God'—and raising his hands to heaven—'who has made
all that!' In all ages and under all conditions the priest was the natural
ally of the civil governor. His duty was to teach the passive virtues, to
discourse upon 'the morality which unites', not upon 'the doctrine
which divides', to help his parishioners by his smattering of law,
agriculture, and medicine, and through the soothing power of his
ministrations to promote the ends of social discipline. 'Fifty *émigré*
bishops in English pay', observed Napoleon, 'are the present leaders
of the French clergy. Their influence must be destroyed, and for this
I must have the authority of the Pope.'

For these among other reasons Napoleon resolved to come to terms
with Rome. The negotiation was conducted in Paris, upon the side
of the Italian cardinals with tenacity and finesse, upon that of
Napoleon with subtlety shading into fraud. At last, in August 1802,
the Concordat was accepted which for a hundred and three years
continued to govern the relations between Church and State in
France. The Pope recognized the constitutional clergy, and reduced
establishment, the revolutionary land settlement. The First Consul
re-established the Catholic Church in France, guaranteed its right
to public worship, and acknowledged it to be the religion of the
majority of Frenchmen. The principle of establishment, then as now,
had many enemies but it is difficult to contest the value of an arrangement which soothed the fears of the peasantry, healed the schism in
the French Church, and, save for an inconsiderable body of non-
jurors, reconciled the Catholic conscience to the government of the
day. 'The altars', in Bonaparte's phrase, 'were restored'; but the
clergy were soon to discovered that they had bought recognition at a
heavy price. By a series of 'organic regulations' suddenly tacked on
to the Concordat they were bound hand and foot, the helpless
instruments of an omnipotent State.

Before this Napoleon had already defined his attitude to that
intractable spirit in politics which is the creature and bequest of
revolution. While everything, from a village mayoralty to a seat in
the Council of State, was open to such members of the Jacobin and
royalist parties as rallied to the Government, the irreconcilable was

thrown beyond the pale of toleration and justice. When, on December 24, 1800, an attempt was made to blow up the First Consul as he drove to the opera, the offence was visited not upon the guilty but undiscovered royalists, but on the extreme members of the Jacobin connexion, who were known to be dangerous and were hastily assumed to be connected with the plot. Without a particle of solid evidence against them a hundred and thirty Jacobins were deported by Napoleon, not so much in expiation of past offences but as a guarantee against future crime. Something may be excused to the man who goes about in constant peril from assassination; but to correct atrocity by injustice is to ignore the alphabet of statesmanship.

The royalist was less dangerous than the Jacobin and far less easy to absorb in the economy of the new state. His capital was London, his sphere of belligerent operations the wild and tangled regions of Western France, his force the allegiance of a desperate peasantry and the sympathy of Catholic men and women all over the world. The first task of the French Republic was to crush the local rising in the Vendée, the second to parry the disjointed blows of a cosmopolitan conspiracy. Concessions upon the point of religion had already brought peace within sight in the west before Napoleon returned from Egypt, and to him, therefore, belong the finishing touches only in the work of conciliation and disarmament. The grand achievement of stilling a struggle characterized throughout by singular ferocity was unfortunately stained by the shadow of a crime. Frotté, the most intrepid and obstinate of the royalist leaders, coming into Alençon under a safe-conduct, was seized, put to the judgement of a military tribunal, and shot with all his staff; we cannot prove an order from Napoleon, but we know that the officer who thus stained the military honour of his country never received a reprimand.

The pacification of the Vendée in 1800 was a truce rather than a settlement. As it became increasingly clear that Napoleon was in no humour to play the role of General Monk, the desperadoes of the royalist party plotted his removal by violent means. The centre of the conspiracy—which was in effect murder under the flimsiest disguise—was the Count of Artois, that prince of the blood whose cowardice, folly, and superstition were evidenced in a long career as dishonourable to himself as it was disastrous to his friends. His principal agents and accomplices were General Pichegru, the conqueror of Holland, and Georges Cadoudal, a typical Chouan hero, who had risked his burly form and bull-neck too often in the ambuscades and *mêlées* of the west to shrink from the crowning peril of an armed affray with Napoleon's escort. But like all conspiracies of a wide design, the scheme was difficult of execution. Before Georges and his Chouans had landed in France the threads of the affair were in the hands of Napoleon's police. They knew how it was intended to kill or take the First Consul in an open *mêlée*, and how it was hoped that Moreau, the most famous of the generals who regretted the advance of despotism, might thereupon be induced to come forward and restore the monarchy. The conspirators, real or assumed, were taken and put upon their trial. For Georges and his twelve hardy fellows death was no unexpected or unmerited retribution. Pichegru died in prison, probably by his own hand. The evidence against Moreau proved him to be the friend of Pichegru, not the accomplice of Georges, but the Pompey of the French Revolution was nevertheless sentenced to imprisonment and then banished to America by the grace of his victorious rival.

So far, despite the boiling up of fierce passions, royalist and republican, things had gone smoothly for Napoleon. He had been greatly wronged. His splendid services to France had been requited by a base and dastardly conspiracy. He had taken a sufficient but not an excessive revenge. But at this point in his career he committed the crime which was worse than a blunder, and the blunder which was worse than a crime. It came out from the trial of Cadoudal that a royal prince was expected in Paris to give a lead to the affair. The police suspected the Duc d'Enghien, a young man then residing at Ettenheim in Baden, just across the French frontier, and falsely reported to be in communication with the traitor Dumouriez. Napoleon ordered his arrest, his trial, and his death. At five o'clock on the evening of March 20, 1804, the prince was brought to Vincennes, and at eleven o'clock put upon his trial. At half-past two in the following morning, with the ink still wet upon his sentence, the last of the Condés, erect, fearless, and innocent, was taken out into the moat, shot down, and thrown into a grave which had been prepared before the officers of the court had completed their hollow inquiry.

In this extraordinary act of precipitate violence Napoleon was governed by a mixture of passion and statecraft. Long before the prince had reached Paris, the evidence which had given rise to the first suspicions of the police was known to be baseless. The prince was a frank enemy, no secret conspirator. He had nothing to do with the plot of which he disapproved. He was not in communication with Dumouriez. His residence near the French frontier was correctly explained by the two cardinal passions of well-born youth, courtship and the chase. Yet knowing his innocence, Napoleon decided that he must be shot, as a warning to the Bourbon family and their supporters no further to dabble in conspiracy. 'These people', he said on the evening of the execution, 'wish to slay the Revolution in my person; it is my duty to defend and avenge it. We have left behind the age of etiquette. I have shed blood. It was my duty. I shall shed more perhaps in future.' The speed and secrecy with which the affair was carried through stifled the monitions of conscience and abridged the appeals of his household. It also added to the awful impressions of the lesson. No prince of the blood ever afterwards attempted to plot Napoleon's murder, princes even having learnt, by this example, how sharp and swift was a Corsican vendetta. The avenger too paid his price, as we learn from those who watched him at the crisis and have reported how a mind, big with impending crime, becomes sombre, irritable, and defiant, chafes against itself and conceives a wrathful suspicion of the world.

The day which opened with this tragedy is memorable in the history of France for the passage into law of the Civil Code. This famous monument of jurisprudence realized the desire, entertained as far back as the fifteenth century and passionately held during the French Revolution, for the priceless boon of legal unity. The members of Napoleon's Council of State worked upon the basis of five draft codes prepared but never executed by the revolutionary assemblies. But if the idea of a single code, brief, clear, and humane, is not original with Napoleon, to him belongs the credit of execution. A period of revolution, when divisions are sharp and beliefs mutable and unsettled, is not well adapted for the task of codification. The golden moment arrives when the storms have cleared away and the grand features of the legal landscape stand out in clear outline. Napoleon seized the occasion. His Code embodies the permanent conquests, while rejecting the temporary extravagances, of the French Revolution. It is founded upon the principles of toleration and equity. It acknowledges divorce and civil marriage. There is no clearer

statement of the sanctity of private property or of the binding value
of family life.

Critics have assailed the Civil Code as a rapid and superficial
structure, as a pocket-handbook indicating some general legal
principles, but far from exhausting the casuistry of life or precluding
the growth of a jungle of case law. The task to which modern Germans devoted fifteen years of exhausting effort, Napoleon dared to
accomplish in four months. His temerity has been censured. Yet,
however imperfect the Civil Code may be, it is better than no code
at all; and had the work not been done when and as it was, France
might be codeless to this day. A single law is better than two hundred
customs, equality is better than privilege. In the compass of a little
volume which may be read and understood by every man and
woman in the country, the Civil Code depicts the outlines of a
civilized and democratic society, adjusting the great body of revolutionary enactment to the old and inveterate traditions of the race.

In the work of discussion and draftsmanship Napoleon took a
prominent part. 'He spoke', says Thibaudeau, 'without embarrassment and without pretension. He was never inferior to any member
of the Council: he often equalled the ablest of them by the ease with
which he seized the point of a question, by the justice of his ideas and
the force of his reasoning; he often surpassed them by the turn of his
phrases and the originality of his expression.' He picked up law, as the
hawk its food, in the intervals of flight. A copy of the Institutes or of
Domat devoured in the guardroom at Valence, a treatise or two
snatched during an Italian campaign, some evening talks with
Tronchet and Portalis, the thirty-five long debates in Council—such
was the source and sum of his legal equipment. There is, however,
no real mystery about law. Bad law may be obscure and difficult,
but good law is organized common sense. Napoleon applied to the
problems of law a grand natural intelligence. He did not view the
code from the angle of the legal profession or ask himself how a new
rule would affect the habits and emoluments of the legal class. He
stood upon the platform of the public interest. He was free alike from
the prejudices of the Churchman, to whom divorce was anathema, and
from those of the revolutionary, who in the name of freedom would
make it as easy to change a wife as a lodging. Certain things he stood
for in virtue of a deep natural instinct fortified by experience—the
subjection of woman, the power of the father, a regulated system of

divorce, the sanctity of private property. Feminists and socialists will therefore find little to applaud in the legal work of Napoleon; nor would he have courted their commendation. The Civil Code belongs to the category not of socialist but of liberal documents, and its importance in the history of civilization lies in the fact that it registers and perpetuates the vast social improvements introduced into Europe by the French Revolution.

5

The Prelude of Empire

THE CIVIL ACHIEVEMENTS of the Consulate, the most dazzling of their kind in the history of Europe, occupied but a part of Napoleon's energy. The four years which in the domestic history of France are marked by the pacification of the Vendée, the Church settlement, and the Civil Code, which witnessed the elevation of France from a state of chaos and distraction to an unparalleled level of prosperity, are also years of crowded diplomacy and brilliant conquests, of far-reaching plans of colonial empire, and of restless machinations to extend French influence in Europe. (The policy of aggression was not the invention of Napoleon, but the bequest of the Revolutionary Government.) Long before the *coup d'état* of Brumaire the diplomatists of the Republic had conceived of their great democracy as girdled with a ring of republican satellites, and as exercising by virtue of its energy and the natural seduction of its institutions an overwhelming influence on Europe. They regarded Belgium and Savoy as integral parts of France; Holland and Switzerland as natural appendages; and Italy as the appointed theatre of revolution to be conducted on the French model and in the French interests. The arrogance of this diplomacy had been duly supported by arms; and for a few months in the early part of 1799 the French had not only secured the Rhine frontier, but had also divided the Italian peninsula into satellite republics. Then, while Napoleon was still absent in Egypt, the tide began to turn. A new coalition was formed on the Continent, and while the armies of Austria successfully ejected the French from Italy, an Anglo-Russian expedition was dispatched to the shores of Holland.

Napoleon's return from Egypt was not, as has been sometimes

assumed, the first gleam of light in a dark horizon. The most pressing danger had been already averted by victories won at Zürich by Masséna and in Holland by Brune; and before Napoleon had stepped upon the quay of Fréjus, Suvaroff, the one living commander whose military intuition might have rivalled his own, was executing a retreat through the snows of Switzerland. Even if Napoleon had been drowned at sea, France would probably have been able to preserve the Rhine frontier, and with it that ascendancy in Europe which she lost at the fall of the Empire and has never since been able to regain. But the significance of Napoleon's sudden intrusion lies in the fact that the natural frontier was not enough for him. No peace would satisfy his ambition which did not at least restore to France that control of northern Italy which had been the fruit of his early victories and the substance of the peace of Campo-Formio. Such a programme could not be imposed upon powers like Austria and England save at the point of the sword, and the proffers of peace which upon his assumption of power the First Consul addressed to George III and Francis II were designed with a view to exploring the ground and to deceiving the public, rather than with any serious expectation that peace would ensue. Nevertheless a small portion of posterity has discovered in these admirable epistles the soul of a peace-lover; and in every generation Bonapartist writers have been found to argue that the most pacific of rulers was drawn into a long course of war and conquest by malignant antagonists and inexorable fate.

Though the coalition had been seriously weakened by the withdrawal of Russia, the military situation at the beginning of 1800 was by no means favourable to France. In Germany indeed the French and Austrian forces were evenly balanced, for the armies of Moreau and Kray which faced each other on the Lower Rhine amounted to 120,000 men; but in Italy the French were at a grave disadvantage, for while Melas had an army 80,000 strong in Piedmont, Masséna who was posted on the Riviera, had 30,000 only under his command. It was therefore not unlikely that while Kray and Moreau balanced each other in Germany, the frontier of Provence would be pierced by an Austrian army co-operating with an English fleet and counting upon the assistance of the Provençal royalists.

The most complete way of countering such an attack would be a crushing French victory on the Rhine. If Kray were annihilated in Southern Germany the road to Vienna would be open to the French, and the Austrians would probably be compelled to evacuate all their advanced positions in Italy. Indeed, as Napoleon afterwards observed, 'In this campaign the frontier of Germany is the decisive point, the littoral of Genoa a secondary one.' In accordance with these views Napoleon, having collected a reserve army equally prepared to assist Masséna and Moreau, originally decided for the German field of operations. His plan was simple and grandiose. He would cross the Rhine at Schaffhausen, suddenly throw himself with a superior force upon Kray's left flank and rear, cut his communications, push him back on the Rhine, and annihilate his army as the Turks were annihilated at Aboukir. When this was done, he would march on Vienna and dictate a peace in the Austrian capital.

An obstacle of a personal nature caused the withdrawal of this scheme. (Moreau felt himself too great to act as Napoleon's subordinate and was too famous to be dismissed.) It was therefore decided in the first week of March that the reserve army should be thrown not into Germany but into Italy, and that while Moreau covered his rear and left flank by an offensive movement south of the Danube, Napoleon should strike across Switzerland, and catching Melas on flank and rear at once relieve the pressure on Masséna, and compel the Austrians to a retreat which would certainly be precipitate, and would probably be disastrous. The manner in which this daring plan was carried out, the secrecy, the dispatch, the detailed finish of the arrangement have deservedly received the applause of posterity, and the seven days' passage of the St. Bernard over a fair road and in the month of May, though far from being the most difficult, is one of the most famous exploits of Napoleon. A matter which more vividly illustrates the military genius of Napoleon than the successful and uncontested passage of a well-known Alpine pass is the simple originality of his general design and the rapidity with which particular parts of it were altered to suit changing circumstances. Thus he originally thought of crossing the Splügen, but, partly owing to Moreau's inaction and partly owing to the intelligence that the Austrians were engaged with Masséna, decided for the St. Bernard, which is 140 miles to the west. Again, once across the pass it was his first intention to march straight upon Melas. But arriving at Ivrea on May 26, he learnt that Masséna was still holding out at Genoa, and in the elation of success substituted for the original plan, which would have allowed his adversary a line of retreat, the more ambitious scheme of a march on Milan, a conquest of Lombardy, and a seizure of the passages on the middle Po. Military critics are divided upon the question whether it is not the first duty of the commander of a relieving army to march to the guns of a beleaguered fortress. Genoa after an heroic defence capitulated on June 4, and Napoleon has been blamed for not averting the catastrophe. But the weight of expert opinion is in favour of the plan which he pursued. The business of a commander is to destroy his enemy rather than to help his friends. By throwing his army across the line of Melas' communications Napoleon adopted a course which, had Genoa not been eating its last crust, would either have drawn the besieging army from its walls or have exposed the Austrian commander to certain destruction at the hands of an army far more numerous than his own. In war, success or failure is often ultimately a matter of imagination, and the sudden apparition of Napoleon in the capital of Lombardy exercised a moral effect over the whole of Italy which may well have been worth the delay which it involved.

In spite of this brilliant prelude the battle of Marengo (June 14, 1800), which crowns the campaign, is memorable as an instance of the errors into which the greatest general may fall through an overdrawn contempt for his enemy. So poor did Napoleon think of the elderly gentleman opposed to him, that, disregarding his own cardinal maxims of war, he started for Alessandria, upon which the Austrians were concentrating, with a force not exceeding 34,000 men. Even these numbers were regarded as an excessive compliment to the enemy, and in the course of the French advance westward 6,000 men were shed to guard Cremona and Piacenza, while another division under the command of the brilliant Desaix was detached to head off a possible retreat to Genoa. Upon the assumption that the main body of the Austrians could make no serious resistance, it was good strategy to beset every possible avenue of escape; but the Austrian is a stubborn fighter, and the prowess of the white-coats on the plain of the Bormida showed the danger of making arrangements for a capture until you have effectually secured a defeat. The battle, which began at daybreak, was in its earlier stages so disastrous to the French that at one o'clock Melas rode back into Alessandria in the full belief that the day was won and that the finishing touches of the pursuit could be delegated to subordinates. Slowly and surely, with many rallies, the French were pushed eastward along the road to San Giuliano, and the rout seemed to have

c

degenerated into a stampede, when about four o'clock in the afternoon Desaix suddenly appeared on the scene. He had heard the guns, and with the instinct of a soldier had marched to the sound without delay. His arrival was the beginning of a rally which converted a disaster into a triumph as decisive as any in military annals. Napoleon was in the village full of resource, energy, and inspiration. 'Children,' he cried, 'remember that it is my habit to sleep on the field of battle.' The men of Desaix's division broke into a charge, supported by the cavalry of Kellermann and the guns of Marmont. Staggered by the unexpected shock the great Austrian column stopped, reeled, and was thrown back in utter confusion across the Bormida. Napoleon slept on the field of battle; so too did Desaix, but his was the sleep of the dead. In the dispatch which records the vulgar trophies of victory, the fifteen flags, the forty guns, the 8,000 prisoners, the 6,000 dead, the First Consul spares a paragraph of genuine lament for the heroic comrade of his Egyptian war. He owed him much, for so shaken was the adversary that on the next day Melas signed an armistice, surrendering all Italy west of the Mincio to the military occupation of the French.

The first political result of this amazing campaign was to give to the Consular Government, while it was still a new and untried experiment, exciting many murmurs and misgivings, that kind of overwhelming prestige which not only silences cavil, but against which even well-founded criticism is at a serious disadvantage. Its second result was to restore the French ascendancy in Italy and to prepare the way for a peace with Austria. Yet since Austria was closely linked with the obstinate power of England, and as yet unbeaten in Germany, she was not prepared to accept Marengo as a compelling motive to a humiliating peace. After a period of international negotiation, conducted with extreme dexterity on the French side, hostilities were resumed on the Continent and brought to a climax on a wintry December day in one of those forest tracts which are characteristic of Bavaria. Moreau's victory at Hohenlinden (December 3, 1800) so fortified the argument grounded on Marengo, that the peace for which France was searching, and which it was the business of Austria, if possible, to avert, was on February 9, 1801, concluded at Lunéville. Again the proud dynasty of the Habsburgs recognized the conquest by France of Belgium, the Rhine frontier, and Savoy. Again it accepted the Batavian, Helvetic, and Cisalpine Republics; and again the Holy

Roman Emperor consented to an internal revolution in Germany in order that a government made possible by regicide and revolution might secure its ill-gotten gains. The Treaty of Lunéville restored the situation which had been won at Campo-Formio, with some modifications all unfavourable to Austria. Never since the great days of Louis XIV had a French diplomatist affixed his signature to a peace so glorious and therefore so unstable.

A different method was necessarily pursued in dealing with the other limb of the anti-Gallican league. Since the French navy was not in a sufficient state of preparedness to encourage a direct invasion, Napoleon set himself to contrive a continental coalition against England. Of this immense confederacy the principal member was to be Paul I, the mad autocrat of Russia, who having take a sudden umbrage against the government of George III on the inadequate ground that it had captured Malta, was prepared to acquiesce in suggestions, however extravagant, for promoting his new and whimsical aversion. In Napoleon's eyes the value of such an alliance bore no proportion to the stability of the Tsar's character and intelligence. 'Russia', he observed on January 2, 1801, 'holds the key of Asia.' Russia's help might enable him to conquer India, to hold Egypt, to take a share of the Balkans; more directly still, through the league of Northern Powers recently organized by the Tsar to dispute the British maritime law, it might shatter the commercial prosperity of England. Round this central understanding with the Tsar, and through him with the maritime powers of Denmark, Prussia, and Sweden, were grouped a number of complementary negotiations and alliances. The weak government of Naples was compelled to exclude English goods and to suffer a French army of occupation to be quartered upon its territory until such time as the French troops could be trans-shipped to Egypt; and Spain was coerced into a similar act of compliance. In return for Tuscany, the corrupt and feeble Government of Charles IV bound itself not only to sell Louisiana to Napoleon but to invade unoffending Portugal, in order that England might be robbed of her last ally and most faithful customer among the continental powers.

The same spring which saw the creation witnessed the sudden dissolution of this extraordinary confederacy. On March 24, Paul was murdered in St. Petersburg and the linchpin fell out of the whole machine. At the same time unpleasant reminders rained down upon

Napoleon of the awkward effects of a navy controlled by a 'nation of shop-keepers'. On March 20, Abercromby won a decisive victory in Egypt. On April 2, Nelson destroyed the Danish fleet at Copenhagen. The First Consul saw, or affected to see, a connecting thread between the explosives which had missed him in Paris, the entry of a British fleet into the Sound, and the murder of the Tsar. 'The English', he observed bitterly, 'missed me on 3 Nivose, they have not missed me at St. Petersburg.' Nevertheless he was impelled by the failure of his diplomatic combinations to contemplate a peace with the Government of assassins. It was clearly to his interest, at whatever temporary sacrifice of ambition, to obtain such a respite as would enable him to repair that fatal deficiency in ships which had lost him Malta and Egypt and twice sheltered his active enemy from invasion. Nothing effectual could be done without a navy, for the league of the Continent against England had broken down. The new Tsar Alexander had accommodated the differences which divided Russia and England, the League of Neutrals was dissolved, and though Portugal had been coerced into the exclusion of English goods, the Spaniards had deeply offended the First Consul by the lack of spirit which they had thrown into the invasion and by their impertinent readiness to conclude a peace. So on October 1, 1801, preliminaries of a treaty between France and England were signed in London.

Five months later these preliminaries ripened into the Peace of Amiens. The interval was employed by Napoleon not in disarming the suspicions of his adversary, but in piling up fresh evidence of his enterprise and power. Even the keenest Whig who followed Fox into the lobbies could not help acknowledging that the philanthropy of Fox's hero did not belong to the Quaker type. He had annexed Piedmont in April, had tightened his hold over the Dutch in September, had constituted an Italian republic (covering the same ground as the old Cisalpine) with himself as omnipotent President in January. From the heel of Italy to the Hook of Holland French troops were quartered upon alien populations, and alien subsidies were pouring into the French treasury. Nor was the First Consul's activity confined to Europe. He had extracted an addition to French Guiana from Portugal, and dispatched a powerful army to recover San Domingo from the negroes. It was plain that he intended to win an empire in the West to balance his exclusion from Egypt and Syria.

By the Treaty of Amiens England abandoned all her colonial

conquests save Ceylon and Trinidad, surrendered Malta to the Knights, restored Minorca to Spain, and dropped the royal title of France, which ever since Edward III had been used by the English kings. To balance these concessions Napoleon agreed to evacuate Egypt, which he could not hold, Naples, which he could always conquer, and Portugal, which had only incurred his animosity as the passive ally of an enemy. Accepted from the first with recrimination in England, the peace was based upon foundations the instability of which became more evident as every week revealed new glimpses of Napoleon's restless ambitions. To English critics the treaty seemed to surrender far more than any British statesman had any right to concede, and to ignore points upon which it was the duty of every patriot to insist. It surrendered the Cape and Martinique; it made no protest against a French Piedmont, a French Lombardy, and a French Holland. Such an arrangement of the world, even if it could ever be made palatable to British ideas, was only to be tolerated if it were accompanied by no further aggravations. The ordinary Englishman did not understand the meaning of a peace which involved no relaxation of commercial duties, no slackening of military preparations, and no intermission of colonial designs. In Napoleon's refusal to consent to a commercial treaty he read an obvious desire to weaken the industrial strength of the island. He could not understand how any country could be the true ally of Great Britain which treated British goods as if they were the tainted product of some plague-stricken ghetto. He distrusted the San Domingo expedition and the Louisiana transfer. He believed that peace had been accepted by Bonaparte with the sole design of building a navy capable of wresting from England her colonies in India and America, and of transporting an army to her shores; and when he read in his newspaper that the First Consul had been giving a constitution to the Swiss or that he had sent a colonel to the Levant upon a political and military mission, he thought that his worst suspicions had been abundantly confirmed.

In the calm evening of his life Napoleon would speak with regret of the British perversity which had stood between Europe and 'moral regeneration'. Yet however much he might profess his pacific intentions at St. Helena, the idea of a stable and permanent peace was never in his mind. He had never for a moment abandoned the project of recovering Egypt, of founding a French power in India, and of shaking the maritime ascendancy of England. In common with the short-lived League of Neutrals he held that it was essential to the progress of civilization that Great Britain should be forced to abandon her claim to search neutral vessels for enemies' goods and to seize neutral vessels trading with enemies' ports. He had always been a strong Protectionist, holding that agriculture is more valuable than manufactures, manufactures than commerce, and being inclined to set no bounds to the power which a government may exert in educating new industries. He was therefore violently opposed to a commercial treaty with England, or to any concession to the 'ideologues' of Free Trade. An autocrat himself, and a past master in the art of disciplining the Press to compliance with autocracy, he could not understand and he bitterly resented the libellous freedom of the London pamphleteer. Already his ideal of Europe as revealed in his chance conversation and correspondence differed widely from any which British statesmen could entertain. He regarded the Mediterranean as strictly belonging to the Latin powers, in other words to France, exercising a constant and guiding pressure upon the dependent peninsulas of Italy and Spain. He thought of Germany as an uncouth federation of venal governments, already more than half enfeoffed to France, and destined in an increasing measure to enjoy the benefits of French direction. Having composed by a brilliant act of statesmanship the intestine feuds of her democrats and federalists, he viewed Switzerland as a satellite. And it belonged to the established economy of his state, that while Holland, Spain, and Genoa should contribute to his navy, the honour of supporting the army of France should be liberally distributed among her allies and dependents.

Such then being Napoleon's general outlook upon the politics of Europe the resumption of the war could not have been long deferred. But to say that a war is inevitable at some time does not imply that the time is indifferent. Napoleon had everything to gain by delay. The conquest of San Domingo, the settlement of Louisiana, not to speak of ulterior plans of colonial development, depended upon the quiescence of the English fleet until such time as the shipwrights of Antwerp, Brest, and Toulon should have brought the French navy to a level with its rival. It is therefore a blot upon Napoleon's prudence, firstly, that he should have embarked upon a great overseas enterprise before his navy had been adequately strengthened; and secondly, that while the fortune of that expedition was in suspense, he should have supplied provocations to the one power capable of completely foiling his design. At St. Helena Napoleon recognized that the expedition to San Domingo was a great mistake. He might have added that he had been expressly warned against the project by the ablest of the local experts. It was not a question of recovering a rebel colony or of composing a civil war in a lucrative possession of the French Republic. San Domingo still flew the French flag and acknowledged the French allegiance. It had, moreover, after a frightful period of distraction, recently been brought under control by the only negro of unmixed blood who had ever exhibited the qualities of a statesman. Toussaint l'Ouverture had given to the island the three principal constituents of its reviving prosperity—a stable supply of black labour on the plantations, a free exchange of commerce with the mainland of America, and a civil service manned by whites. The First Consul would have done wisely to accept his work.

There is nothing more terrible in the world than the colour feeling of America when it is fevered by panic or disaster. The white planters, who had fled from San Domingo in the servile war, represented that it was intolerable for a great French colony, the pearl of all the sugar islands, to be under the heel of a sanctimonious negro and his formidable array of grinning blacks. And since it was equally contrary to Napoleon's ideas that a colony of France should presume to buy its necessaries from America and its luxuries from London, a case was soon made out for the destruction of Toussaint. The army of San Domingo was entrusted to General Leclerc, husband of Pauline Bonaparte, and the brother-in-law of Napoleon; and since it had served with Moreau on the Rhine, it was surmised by the more cynical observers of the First Consul's methods that the expedition was designed for the banishment of his domestic opponents. A more certain ground for censure is supplied by the secret instructions given to the general-in-chief. Leclerc was commanded to cajole, trap, and deport the dictator and his generals, to destroy the negro army, and then to restore slavery in the eastern part of the island. The first part of the programme was accomplished; and having been seized by an act of execrable treachery, Toussaint was sent to die among the icy blasts of Jura. His tragedy, which inspired Wordsworth with a famous sonnet, brought no luck to its contriver. The yellow fever swooped down like an avenging spirit upon the brilliant army of San Domingo, and had reduced it to a helpless and miserable fragment when the reopening of the war with England abruptly closed the western world to Napoleon's ambition.

The peace was broken upon the point of Malta. To England, preoccupied above all things with India, it seemed to be a vital necessity that this small island in the Mediterranean with its noble harbour and splendid fortress should on no account be liable to a second seizure by the French. By the terms of the treaty the independence of the island was to be guaranteed by six great powers, and upon that guarantee being obtained, it was to be evacuated by the British troops and garrisoned by Neapolitans for a period of three years, at the conclusion of which it was assumed that the Knights of St. John might be able to provide for its defence. If Napoleon had consented to intermit his designs upon the East, it is safe to assume that no difficulties would have arisen with regard to Malta. The British troops would have been promptly withdrawn, the Neapolitans would have been replaced, and the treaty would have been satisfied in letter and spirit. But Napoleon was constitutionally incapable of soothing the susceptibilities of his rivals. At the very moment when naval and military interests demanded a long peace with England, his conduct was so framed as to excite the liveliest apprehensions of all the powers who were interested in the eastern littoral of the Mediterranean. He spoke to the Tsar of the partition of Turkey, and of the Morea as a territory well-suited to the French. He equipped (January 1803) an expedition to India. The loss of Egypt and Syria touched him so deeply that he wasted no time in dispatching a mission to explore the means for their recovery. The English government, which had already been implored by the Porte to hold on to Malta, found in the mission of Colonel Sebastiani an additional reason for suspecting Napoleon, and when on January 30, 1803, the report of the mission appeared in the *Moniteur*, depicting the popularity of the French in the Levant and the ease with which Egypt might be reconquered, the Cabinet resolved that Malta must continue to be held by English troops until the country was reassured as to Egypt and Turkey. We need not discuss the technical issues. On the face of it England, by refusing to withdraw, had violated the treaty. And though it might be argued that some of the conditions precedent to evacuation had not been executed, England's real justification rests not upon technical grounds, but on the fact that the unimpeded activity of Napoleon was no longer compatible with her place in the world.

To Talleyrand, the French foreign minister who was working for peace, the chief obstacle appeared to be the wounded *amour propre* of the First Consul. Lord Whitworth, the British Ambassador in Paris, reported after a two hours' interview that Napoleon talked more like a captain of dragoons than as the head of a great state. Gusts of pride, temper, and arrogance constantly swept him from the even course. In moments of equilibrium he would speak of ten years of peace as essential to procure the means of mastering the ocean; but there were other moments, and these not infrequent, when he would lash himself up into fury, saying that he could call out, if need be, two million troops, that he was not afraid of a fight, that nothing would induce him to surrender a point in the treaty to the arrogant John Bull, that the English could do him little harm, that they might take a couple of frigates and a few colonies, but that he would carry the terrors of war to London. 'If the first war', he remarked in April, 'has brought in Belgium and Piedmont, the second will establish our federal system even more securely.'

He was not then afraid of a rupture which would lead to fresh conquests on the Continent, cover up the San Domingo disaster, and give a new turn to the energies of France. By a plausible system of casuistry he persuaded himself that war and tyranny were essential to the stability of a power founded on revolution and exposed to the jealousies which are engendered by civil strife. 'My position', he would say, 'is entirely different from that of the old sovereigns. They can live a life of indolence in their castles and surrender themselves without shame to every kind of vice. Nobody contests their legitimacy, nobody thinks of replacing them; nobody accuses them of being ungrateful, because nobody has helped to raise them to the throne. Everything is different in my case. There is not a general who does not think that he has the same right to the throne as I. There is not a man who does not believe that he shaped my course on the 18th Brumaire. . . . I am therefore obliged to be very severe to these men. . . . Within and without, my dominion is founded on fear. If I abandoned the system I should be immediately dethroned.' With such ideas fermenting in his mind Napoleon, while still with the more reasonable part of him desiring to postpone the rupture, and even offering some concessions to England, eagerly pushed on preparations for war.

The great duel of the nineteenth century, which was finally closed on the field of Waterloo, opened on May 16, 1803. In a superb message to the Senate Napoleon spoke of the moderation and patience of French diplomacy, of the exorbitant claims of England, of the justice of his cause and the courage of his warriors. His scheme of operations was an invasion preceded and supported by a rigorous exclusion of British merchandise from the territory of the Republic and her allies. At least he was under no illusions as to the magnitude of the struggle in which he was now involved. 'This war', he said in May, 'will naturally entail a war on the Continent: to meet this I must have upon my side Austria or Prussia.' And since he reckoned that he could easily win Prussia 'by giving her a bone to gnaw', and that Russia would be 'always inactive', he set his plans to face a possible struggle with the old enemy whom he had twice victoriously confronted amid the mountains and plains of Italy.

England and Austria, Austria and England—as in the days of Marlborough and Eugène, these powers were still the inveterate enemies of French expansion, the one barring the way on the Continent of Europe, the other besetting the ocean pathways to the world beyond.

6

The Conquests of Empire

THE DISCOVERY AND PUNISHMENT of the royalist plot in March 1804 hastened the completion of a project which had long been maturing in Napoleon's mind, and for two years at least had been a matter of public speculation. The First Consul had never been content with a constitution under which his office was limited to a term of ten years, and his power checked, however slightly, by the action of parliamentary bodies. Such a position was not adequate to the deserts of a man who already aspired to the fame of an Alexander, a Charlemagne, or a Caesar. Accordingly, in 1802, the French people were asked to decide whether Napoleon Bonaparte should be Consul for life; and the overwhelming affirmative of their reply led to a considerable extension of his powers. On August 4, 1802, Napoleon was given the right to name his successor, and to fill the Senate with his own nominees. And since the Tribunate was reduced to fifty members and the electoral colleges were named for life, the last vestige of freedom was eliminated from the State. The new decree was the act of the Senate, a body which had been entrusted with the special charge of guarding the constitution, and was now and henceforth the compliant agent of its destruction. Of opposition there was no sign, for to facilitate the passage of the bill the courtyard and corridors of the Luxembourg Palace were by a characteristic but unnecessary measure of precaution filled with grenadiers.

It implied no great change either in the state of public opinion or in the mind of Bonaparte when in March 1804 the life consulate gave way to an hereditary empire. Great as was the shock caused by the execution of the Duc d'Enghien, it was overwhelmed by the reflection of the terrible calamities in which France would be involved if the head of the state were to fall by the hand of an assassin. It should be remembered that Napoleon had saved France from anarchy, and that he had given her a government which by every test that could be applied was likely, if not overset by some violent catastrophe, to be as stable as it was glorious. His life and his life alone stood between France and civil war. There were many Frenchmen who deplored the loss of liberty, many who regretted the renewal of the war, and not a few who had already conceived a deep distrust of Napoleon's methods and ambitions. But even these, however much they were inclined to grumble at tyranny, and to find in Moreau their archetype of political virtue, had no taste for the renewal of the Vendée or the Terror. They felt that it was high time that foreign intriguers should be instructed that France had, once and for all, made election of the government which suited her peculiar needs, and that since the removal of Napoleon would not alter the situation, neither *émigré* nor terrorist had anything to gain by removing him.

The difficulties attending the foundation of the Empire came neither from the French people nor from the Chambers, but from the inner circle of Napoleon's family. Senate, tribunate, legislature were ready to swallow the principle of an hereditary autocracy which twelve years before had been violently discarded; and even in the Council of State, so rich in revolutionary characters, there were but seven dissentient voices. In the eyes of the peasantry, the soldiers, and the middle class anything was preferable to a new revolution, or to the disturbance of a settlement based on equality. The sole difficulty came from the fact that since no children were borne by Josephine, the succession to the Empire was an open question which could not be debated without cabal or closed without heartburning. The three elder brothers of Napoleon, all men above the ordinary standard of ability, had by this time shot up into positions of affluence and splendour; and though they differed from one another in important points of temperament, Louis being as chilly as Lucien was hot, they united in the family characteristics of the jealous temper and the obstinate will. In deference to the strong pressure of Joseph, Napoleon abandoned the Roman and congenial plan of an unlimited right of adoption. The Imperial dignity was not to pass beyond the sacred circle of the sons of Letizia, and failing an heir to the body of the Emperor, or his adoption of a nephew, the crown was to go to Joseph and his heirs, and then to Louis. Two brothers were excluded from the succession, and for the same reason. The headstrong Lucien had contracted a marriage with a woman of the middle class to whom he was deeply attached and whom he honourably refused to abandon; and Jérôme, the Benjamin of the family, had been guilty of a similar imprudence. To the deep anger of Napoleon, to whom every Bonaparte was now a French prince and a possible husband of foreign princesses, the young sailor announced that he had been married in Baltimore, and that he proposed to return to Europe with an American wife.

A necessary complement to the assumption of the Imperial crown was the formation of a regular court and an increased attention to etiquette. Polished ladies and gentlemen who were familiar with the easy graces of Versailles found a subject for mockery in the abrupt manners of the Corsican Emperor and the awkward and ignorant movements of his satellites. Napoleon had made no sacrifices to the graces, and was deficient in all the minor arts of the European aristocracy. His dancing was clumsy, his horsemanship indifferent, and he had none of the instincts and tastes of a sportsman. Occasionally he would follow the hounds, but as a duty owing to his station rather than as a pleasure; or fire at his wife's tame birds in the garden, obeying the same nervous impulse which led him to hack chairs and tables with his penknife and to rend and tear any minor articles which might come to his hand. His musical taste was rudimentary and untrained. He had no care for pictures, nor patience with the superfluous delicacies of social intercourse. Talleyrand, who had known the finished and pleasant courtesies of the *ancien régime*, said that to amuse Napoleon was 'amuser l'inamusable', and that the man treated civilization as his personal enemy. The bitter jibe gave joy to many a delicate lady, who had writhed as the Emperor pulled her ear, or maliciously recounted the rumoured infidelities of her husband. There is nothing more devastating to pleasure than a savage and intolerant relevance; and the conversation of Napoleon, when it was not a brilliant monologue or a sharp reprimand, was apt to be a fatiguing and relevant interrogatory. A court governed by a laborious egoist may have many virtues. It may be economical, it may be raised above the influence of female intrigue, it may be filled not by feeble and amiable parasites but by the statesmen and soldiers of an empire; but it will not be amusing. And the court of the Empire, which had all these merits, as it became more splendid, more stiff

more ceremonial, became less amusing. At its centre was a man to
whom the whole apparatus of court ceremonial—the levée, the
uniforms, the bowings, and the scrapings—was merely an instrument
of government, pleasant only as ministering to his own sense of
power, valuable only as impressing the ordinary human imagination
with the dignity which attaches to the head of the state. The conception of a monarch as a being whose principal function is to please his
subjects was quite alien to Napoleon. His duty and absorbing
pleasure was to rule them, and to rule them always. If he played cards
or chess, he played for victory; if he could not win by fair means, he
cheated. And the spirit of dominion was so much a part of his nature
that no letters, however private, were safe from his inquisition; and,
on every abatement in the pressure of public affairs, he was capable
of prescribing to some lady of the court the size of her family, or the
cost of her kitchen and stables.

This spirit of dominion, so injurious to free and pleasant intercourse, was specially exemplified in Napoleon's treatment of his own
family. He cherished for his mother, his brothers, and his sisters a
real affection, and there is no part of his career more truly honourable
than the privations which he endured in youth, or than the generosity
which he displayed in manhood that he might assist the fortunes of
his family. It was part of the clan-feeling of the Corsican, part also
of his own acute punctilio, to see that his kinsfolk were duly cared
for, and to demonstrate to France and to the world that, family
for family, Bonaparte was better than Bourbon. The foundation of
the Empire opened out an opportunity larger than any which had yet
presented itself of demonstrating this thesis. The Bourbons had
ruled in France, and were still ruling in Spain and Naples: a stock
primarily French, but by force of diplomatic and military prudence
become the symbol of monarchy among the Latin races. A destiny
no less august might be reserved for the sons of Letizia. It would be
a fine adventure, excellent fun, a beautiful demonstration of how the
slow old world may be turned inside out by a man of genius, to make
of them princes, dignitaries, kings in an empire as wide as that of
Charlemagne. But one inexorable condition was attached. Promotion
could only be purchased and station preserved by implicit obedience
to the head of the family.

Ever since the declaration of war with England Napoleon had been
engaged in preparing for an invasion. 'The Channel', he said, 'is a

ditch which needs but a pinch of courage to cross.' And once crossed he reckoned that England would be at his feet. Talking afterwards at St. Helena, he said that four days would have brought him to London, that he would have entered the English capital 'not as a conqueror but as a liberator, a second William III, but more generous and disinterested than he'; and that after proclaiming a Republic he would have dissolved the Peers, reformed the Commons, and distributed the wealth of the patriotic aristocracy among the poor. The *canaille* would have welcomed him; he would have promised 'everything' to the sailors; a separate Republic would have been set up in Ireland; and so the two islands, the one repressed by an alien race, the other by a tyrannous oligarchy, would have shared the regeneration of France.

No value can be attached to these gasconades. Had England been really conquered by Napoleon there is no reason to doubt that her fate would have been similar to that of Prussia after Jena, that she would have been bled white by French tax-collectors, that she would have been saddled with an army of occupation, and that at no very short interval tax-collectors and soldiers would have been driven out of the country by a national rising. A distinguished military writer from the Continent gives it as his opinion that it was a misfortune for Europe that the tricolour never waved over the Tower of London and Windsor Castle, arguing that if Napoleon had conquered England, his power to damage the Continent would have been proportionately weakened, and that England would never have been able to acquire that colonial monopoly which not unnaturally exasperated her continental rivals. It is not perhaps a wild paradox to argue that if a French army had landed in England, the ascendancy of Napoleon in Europe would have been terminated sooner than actually proved to be the case; though a great preponderance of argument is on the other side. But history cannot doubt that it was better for the progress of the world that the greatest share of the colonies should have come under the control of a power believing in political and industrial freedom, rather than of a power or combination of powers practising monopoly. Nor is there any reason for thinking that, however much crippled England might have been by Napoleon, she would not have been able at his fall so rapidly to recover her commerce and marine as to outstrip in the race of colonial dominion countries whose interests were still exclusively or mainly fixed on the continent of

Europe. The downfall of England in 1804 or 1805 might have been the means of restoring Ceylon and the Cape to the Dutch, but it would not have contributed a year to the life or an acre to the size of the colonial empire of Germany.

(For the invasion of England there are three prime essentials—a powerful army, an adequate system of transports, and a navy sufficiently strong to protect the passage and disembarkation of the troops) Of these essentials none was easy to provide, but the first was easier than the second, and the second than the third. In virtue of the conscription and the ruthless operations of the prefects who enforced it, Napoleon was able between May 1803 and May 1805 to raise an army of 210,000 men. The operation was painful and its results were at first far from satisfying. 'A fifth of the conscription', said the emperor, 'is composed of the scum of the nation.' By degrees this army of conscripts, drawn mainly from the poor of the towns and from the honest folk of the country, was hammered into shape by its able and experienced officers, in the great camps of exercise which were established along the coasts of the North Sea and the Channel; and it would have been easy for Napoleon at any time in 1804 or 1805 to have dispatched to the shores of Kent a striking force of 100,000 men, as hardy and expert as any corps which served in the wars of that age.

To furnish adequate transport for such an army was a matter of greater difficulty. Orders were issued in May for 210, in July for 1,410, in August for 2,000 flat-bottomed boats, and a vigorous effort was made to impress upon the people of France the desirability of voluntary contributions. But apart from the impossibility of building so great a number of vessels without blocking all work upon the men-of-war, there was the extreme unlikelihood that they could be convoyed from the ports of building to the port of departure without grievous loss from English cruisers. Napoleon's estimate of what could be done was greatly in excess of what was actually accomplished. The number of craft of all kinds collected in the neighbourhood of Boulogne never reached 1,500, and though the harbour of Boulogne had been enlarged, it was still far too small to admit of an embarkation on less than five or six tides.

(Inadequate and vulnerable as these provisions were, it was the lack of the third essential which proved the fatal flaw in the enterprise.) In the autumn of 1803 Napoleon seems to have thought that he might slip across the Channel, on some dark still night, with little or no assistance from a protecting fleet. Such a scheme was an invitation to disaster. It took no account of the perplexing tides of the Channel, of the narrow exit of Boulogne, and of the difficulty of keeping together a great mass of vessels, mostly keelless, should a breeze spring up in the night. Even if, according to the design then sketched out, a Dutch fleet had sailed with transports from the Texel and a French fleet had dashed out from the Breton harbours to raise war in Ireland, the flotilla would have been helpless without an escort of men-of-war. Napoleon came to see that the necessary preliminary to success was a naval concentration in the Channel. If he could collect in the narrow straits a French fleet which for a space of a few days was stronger than any English fleet which could be brought against it, then the flotilla would pass. But it was just here that the difficulty lay. The French fleet, greatly inferior in calibre and numbers to the British, was widely scattered through the Mediter-ranean, the Biscay, and the Channel ports. The largest contingent was blockaded in Brest harbour, night and day, winter and summer, foul weather and fair weather, by that inflexible sailor Admiral Cornwallis, and though so exact a system of surveillance was no part of his plan, Nelson was in attendance on the Toulon squadron. Confronted by this perplexing situation, only to be resolved if the English admirals could be drawn off from their proper work and enticed into distant waters, Napoleon showed the fertility and daring of a great naval strategist. Feints to Egypt, to Ireland, to the West Indies, the bringing of the Toulon fleet into Cherbourg harbour past Cornwallis and his blockaders after a series of feints on a gigantic scale—his profuse plots bewilder with their ingenuity and air of confidence. In an age of steam, and with the help of bold admirals and expert sailors, some of these plans might have been executed with precision(but Napoleon asked too much of a deficient and crestfallen service, and forgot that the tides and winds do not manoeuvre to the word of command.)

It has sometimes been alleged that all these elaborate schemes and combinations were themselves feints, and that Napoleon never intended to cross the Channel. Nobody who has read the vast, minute, and eager correspondence which for three years revolves round the naval problem can for a moment doubt but that Napoleon was in earnest in his designs for the invasion of England, or that he intended to carry out the project on at least two occasions in the autumn of 1803, in the summer of 1804, and most probably also in the spring and summer of 1805. If the plan was never serious, why was a medal ordered to be struck representing Hercules strangling a mermaid and bearing the legend *Descente en Angleterre, frappé à Londres 1804*? Or why did the Emperor spend five weeks on the north coast in the summer of 1804, throwing the whole weight of his fiery energy into the naval preparations, and taking a strange exhilaration and excitement from the movement of the sea? If nothing serious were intended it is difficult to believe that twenty million francs would in March 1805 have been appropriated to the improvement of the roads in Picardy, or that an elaborate plan should have been projected, upon which there was much subsequent embroidery, for a concentration of all the French squadrons at Martinique, in order that, having drawn the English off the scent, they might suddenly race back across the Atlantic to Boulogne. It was easy and natural to declare that the invasion had never been intended, when it was clear that the plan would not be carried through. Then Napoleon represented in Olympian language that the Channel crossing was never more than the convenient pretext under which the army destined for a continental campaign could be mobilized, maintained, and perfected without offence, that the millions expended on the flotilla, the roads, and the harbours were dust thrown into the eyes of the foreigner, and that the weapon which had been so studiously pointed at England was devised for the confusion of another country at the opposite end of Europe.

In this apology there is just a sediment of truth, inasmuch as, the prospect of a war upon the Continent being always present to Napoleon's mind, the army of Boulogne was capable of being used in one of two ways: either, best of all, against London, or, should the naval combination fail, against the league of mainland powers which Pitt was certain sooner or later to call into existence. Indeed, if England could not be invaded, there were only two means of effectually bringing her to reason—a stroke at India or a continental blockade. In 1798 Napoleon had tried the first course. After the breach of the Treaty of Amiens his mind was principally concerned with the second. To conquer England it might be necessary to conquer Europe; and should the invasion of this island hang fire, it was well to educate some continental quarrel to the point at which a rupture might be easily provoked.

In this art of provocation Napoleon had nothing to learn from history. The court of Vienna, overwhelmed by a succession of military disasters, was prepared to swallow many humiliations before it would be drawn into a new fight. Without the faintest murmur it saw Hanover invaded, Naples reoccupied, Spain coerced to a money subsidy. It accepted in a mood of passive indignation the seizure of a French prince on Imperial territory and his summary execution after a secret trial. When Napoleon assumed the Imperial title it acquiesced; when by a refinement of domination he travelled to Aix-la-Chapelle, the old capital of Charlemagne, in order there to receive the letters from Austria acknowledging his dignity, it acquiesced also. Their highest military experts told the Austrians that they were not ready, and the prudent opinion of the Archduke Charles for many months overbalanced the rasher counsels of the firebrands.

From this attitude of passive acquiescence Austria was rudely disturbed by the proceedings of Napoleon in Italy. Here the House of Habsburg had already been compelled to accept a series of most unpalatable changes. It had seen a republic in Lombardy founded at its expense in 1797, restored at its expense in 1800, and two years later reconstituted in a stronger and more menacing form under the presidency of Napoleon. These operations it had been obliged to condone in the unreal hope that the 'Italian Republic' might act as some kind of buffer between the French in Piedmont and the Austrians in Venice. But in 1804 a new and alarming project was suddenly thrown out. Napoleon declared that it was incompatible with his new position as Emperor to retain the presidency of a republic. Austria was accordingly informed that the Italian Republic had been converted into an hereditary monarchy, that the throne had been accepted by Joseph Bonaparte, under adequate security that the crowns of Italy and France should never be united on a single head. Doubtful as this proposal was, it was soon replaced by a scheme infinitely more disconcerting to the Austrians. The announcement of Joseph's acceptance proved to be precipitate. On closer inspection that prudent and wealthy person, standing in the line of succession to the French Empire, did not care to exchange a comfortable expectation at home for a laborious and responsible exile in Lombardy. For a time Napoleon entertained the idea of adopting the eldest son of his brother Louis, and of conferring upon a boy of three the titular sovereignty of Italy. But this scheme encountering opposition from the father, the Emperor fell back upon a resolution which revealed more clearly the span of his ambition. (He would wear the Italian crown himself.) He would be King of Italy, his stepson Eugène Beauharnais acting as Viceroy in Milan. The arrangement would be temporary, a transitional kingship, pending the evacuation of Malta by the Briton and of Corfu by the Muscovite. But no political observer of competence believed in these professions and safeguards, or thought that it was in the psychology of Napoleon to resign a crown. Indeed the Emperor threw no veil on his intentions. He was the new Charlemagne, lord of Aix-la-Chapelle and of Milan, controlling Gaul and Italy, freshly crowned and anointed Emperor of the French by the Pope of Rome. In June 1805 he proceeded to Italy, crowned himself solemnly with the iron crown of the Lombard Kings in the Cathedral of Milan, even as in the Middle Ages the Holy Roman Emperors would come riding at the head of their German chivalry over the Brenner to affirm their visionary rights over the Lombard plain. Napoleon's powers were fuller and less contested than Barbarossa's; and during the course of his Italian visit he took occasion to create 'an Imperial fief' for his sister Elise at Piombino, and to annex to the French Empire the convenient littoral of the Ligurian Republic.

While Austria was thus directly challenged in Italy, she was urgently pressed to take up the glove by Russia and England. The Tsar Alexander, a young, generous, and ambitious prince, had, under the lively impression of the d'Enghien execution, signed (Nov. 6, 1804) a defensive treaty with Austria to be enforced in the event of new encroachments on the part of France. Those encroachments had now been made: the Treaty of Lunéville had been flagrantly ruptured, and it was represented to the court of Vienna that if she did not act, and act promptly, she would get no men from Russia and no subsidies from England. On June 7, 1805, Francis joined the coalition and began to mobilize his army. The step did not escape the vigilance of Napoleon; but since some months would probably elapse before the Austrians were ready to take the field, he continued to elaborate his last great plan against England. Should that plan miscarry, he would come down like an avalanche on the hasty levies of the Emperor.

'My fleet', he wrote from Boulogne to Talleyrand on August 23, 'left Ferrol with thirty-four ships; it had no enemies in sight. If it obeys its orders and joins that of Brest and enters the Channel, there is still time; I am master of England.' If not, 'I strike my camp here, and on the 23rd of September I shall be in Germany with 200,000 men, and in the kingdom of Naples with 25,000 men. I shall march to Vienna and not hold my hand till I am master of Naples and Venice, and have so increased the dominions of the Elector of Bavaria as to leave me nothing further to fear from Austria.' Now on August 15, Admiral Villeneuve, commanding the allied French and Spanish fleets, had given up the game and put back to Cadiz.

The first object having been thus frustrated by the vigilance of the English navy, it remained for Napoleon to execute the grand alternative. With some lack of calculation the Austrians had determined to throw the bulk of their army into Italy, and to operate in Southern Germany with 50,000 men alone; but this error was far exceeded by the impatience which refused to await the arrival of Russian supports. Though it had been arranged that 50,000 Russians should reach Braunau on the Inn[1] on October 20, General Mack, the Austrian commander, thought it wise to press on towards the French frontier, partly that he might sway the Southern Germans to his side, and partly in the wilder hope that his arrival in France might be the signal for a domestic rebellion. The error met with prompt retribution. While Mack was dreaming of an uncontested progress through the Black Forest, an army three times the strength of his own, better led, better officered, and better disciplined, was racing across Germany over different routes and by stages marked with mathematical precision. With a sure and rapid movement the net was drawn round the unsuspecting quarry; and three weeks after the Grand Army had crossed the Rhine, Mack and his Austrians capitulated at Ulm. 'My plan', wrote the Emperor, 'was carried out exactly as I conceived it'; and perhaps there is no instance, even in the military career of Moltke, when the execution of a great enveloping operation has so closely corresponded to its original design.

While the Russians and Austrians were retreating before Napoleon's advance a storm-cloud was slowly brewing up in the north of Germany. The Prussian Government was then a very different affair from the formidable instrument which later directed the energies of fifty million disciplined and patriotic Germans. Falling short in wealth and population even of the humble standards of

[1] See map, p. 107.

modern Ireland, Prussia seemed under the feeble and unimaginative rule of Frederick William III to have discarded the ambitions of a first-class power. For the last ten years she had pursued a steady system of neutrality, without courage or clairvoyance, and in spite of provocations calculated to sting a spirited people into action. But there were limits even to Prussian patience, and in the autumn of 1805 these limits were reached. With a cool assurance of impunity a section of the French army had marched through Prussian ground on its way to Ulm. If such crimes were left unpunished what was the value of that neutral zone of which Prussia, in virtue of the Treaty of Basle, was the official protector? King and Tsar concerted a treaty alliance at Potsdam. Prussia should offer her armed mediation to Napoleon. Her terms were meant to lead to war after the month's delay adjudged to be necessary for the oiling of the military machine, for she proposed to require of the victor of Ulm that he should withdraw from Holland, Germany, Naples, Switzerland, and Piedmont on pain of finding 180,000 Prussians flung against his long line of communications.

Common prudence should have suggested to the Emperors of Austria and Russia that it would be well to defer a general engagement until such time as the Prussian army had taken the field. Everything, in fact, was to be gained by delay, everything might be lost by a precipitate battle. The French Emperor, though master of Vienna, was exposed to a converging attack from the Archduke Charles, who was hurrying up from Italy, from the Russian army which had fallen back into Bohemia, and was attracting to itself such Austrian detachments as had succeeded in extricating themselves from the death-trap of Ulm. If to these formidable though scattered units there was added the weight of a Prussian army, operating on the middle Danube, the position of Napoleon in Moravia would become untenable. Indeed the Emperor of the French was so fully alive to the perils of the situation that he made overtures successively to Francis and Alexander in the hopes of breaking their accord. He was relieved from his embarrassments not by diplomacy, but by the obliging vanity of the Tsar. Believing that he could beat Napoleon, and anxious to make the glory all his own, Alexander was determined to force on a general engagement. It was on December 2, 1805, the anniversary of Napoleon's coronation, that the great battle was fought which takes its name from the Moravian village of Austerlitz where the allied Emperors had established their headquarters. An amazing spirit of light-hearted confidence reigned in the bivouacs of the French, and on the eve of the battle the frosty night was illumined by a torchlight dance of 70,000 men acclaiming the Emperor and promising him victory on the morn. The allied army, some 80,000 strong, was posted on the heights of Pratzen, ground which Napoleon had already explored, and as the sun rose the enemy could be seen moving down from the plateau 'like a torrent rushing to the plain'. Napoleon's plan was to draw the weight of the Russian attack against his right wing, which was so disposed as to invite it, and then to launch a superior force against the heights of Pratzen and break the Russian centre. The operations were timed with the nicety requisite to military success. 'How long will it take you to reach the heights of Pratzen?' asked the Emperor of Soult. 'Less than twenty minutes,' was the Marshal's reply. 'In that case,' said the Emperor, 'we can wait another quarter of an hour.' When the rattle of musketry and boom of the guns showed that his right was engaged, Napoleon launched Murat, Bernadotte, and Soult against the allied centre. The enemy fought with that Russian courage which has more than once claimed the admiration of history, but was overborne by the weight and dash of the antagonist. By noon Soult was master of the heights, and as the broken remnants of Kutusoff's army were streaming down the northern slopes of the plateau the French centre wheeled round to the right and threw itself upon the flank and rear of the Russian left. The Emperor viewed from the chapel of St. Anthony the envelopment and destruction of three Russian columns, and when the last shots had been exchanged, and in the gathering dusk of a winter evening, rode over the field, noting with a strange curiosity the silent or agonized trophies of the day.

At this terrible stroke the war suddenly stopped. The crestfallen Tsar removed himself to the north and Haugwitz, the Prussian envoy, who had been kept dangling in Vienna while the fate of Europe was hanging in the balance, was sternly compelled at Pressburg to put his name to an ignominious peace. The heaviest retribution fell upon Austria, which now for the third time experienced the wrath of Napoleon. By the Treaty of Schönbrunn, December 26, 1805, Francis signed away the fair provinces of Venice, Istria, and Dalmatia, the mountain bastion of the Tyrol, and those scattered lands in south-western Germany which were among the oldest possessions of the Habsburg house.

Austerlitz made Napoleon supreme in Italy and southern Germany. In the first of these countries he had hitherto been confronted by three alien territories, Venice, Rome, Naples, each inconsiderable in itself, but deriving from the moral and military support of Austria a title to be treated with a certain measure of caution. Having deleted one Austrian army at Ulm and broken part of another at Austerlitz, Napoleon was able to pounce upon the possessions and allies of the Habsburg house in Italy. He incorporated Venice in his Italian kingdom, sent Masséna to hunt the Bourbons out of Naples, and abruptly required the Pope to join the continental blockade. To the demurs of the Curia he answered that he was Emperor of Rome and temporal head of the Church. Italy was his, and that it might be more securely held, the command of the Tyrolese passes was given to the faithful Bavarian ally, who received a crown and a son-in-law as a reward for his assistance in the campaign. The new janitor of Italy would be loyal to his trust, for his daughter, the bride of Eugène, was sent to hold court in Milan.

By these drastic measures the malign and blighting influence of Austria was for eight years excluded from Italy. In that critical and most formative period of her growth Italy received both weal and woe from the hand of her powerful conqueror. Her sons were swept off to fight alien wars; her picture galleries were rifled; her treasuries were drained by the fiscal agents of a military tyranny, but at least she won from the government of Napoleon what the Austrians never could give her, a measure of national hope, a fresh outlook into the modern world, and the elements of a strenuous education in public affairs.

It was one of the peculiar advantages incidental to Napoleon's position that, being the autocrat of France, he could at any moment, and without the least delay, diplomatize to further his military ends. He had not entered the late campaign without first carefully exploring the political ground in Germany. He saw that the South German powers were deeply apprehensive of Austrian ambition, and that by ministering to their selfish greed he could coerce them into an alliance with France. Baden, Würtemberg, and Bavaria were swept along in the French current, signed treaties with Napoleon, and shared in the Austerlitz campaign. After the victory they claimed and received the lands and dignities with which such services are rewarded. The bargain was not one-sided. With incredible rapidity Napoleon, the

king-maker, extorted three children from the obliged potentates—
one for a stepson, a second for the first cousin of a step-daughter,
and a third for his brother Jérôme; and by these amazing though not
unhappy marriages gave to his own gigantic adventure a certain seal
of respectability, and to three ancient but not too glorious lines an
alien touch of romance.[1]

These alliances concluded and confirmed, the way was prepared
for a last shattering blow at Austrian prestige in Germany. In June
1806 Napoleon abolished the Holy Roman Empire, and for that
ancient, ineffective, and very German institution substituted a highly
effective but most unpatriotic league of princes, dependent on himself
and pledged to give definite military support to the French Empire.
The Confederation of the Rhine, as this league is called, is an
astonishing testimony to the helplessness into which a civilized people
may allow itself to drift through centuries of unclear thinking and
misplaced sentiment in politics. Napoleon, who could neither talk
nor read a word of German, had sounded the depth of German
weakness. He wanted German men and German money. Of the
Teutonic literature, if we except *Werther*, which was devoured in a
French translation, he knew nothing, and in his contemptuous
catalogue of the useless dreamers and impostors of the world he
placed with confidence the name of Kant.

Meanwhile the old problem of meting out punishment to 'the
cowardly oligarchs of London' had lost none of its insistency. An
invasion was out of the question. The idea had been abandoned in
August and the battle of Trafalgar effectually precluded its resumption. Napoleon fell back upon a scheme of which some foretaste had
already been given not only in his own earlier policy, but also in that
of the Directory. He determined to close the ports of Europe to
English and Colonial wares. The execution of this gigantic plan,
though it implied a dominion so wide and weighty that the annals
of Asiatic tyranny must be searched for a parallel, never gave him an
instant's pause. He saw, with the geometrical, ruthless lucidity which
is the characteristic of his mind, a whole continent obedient to his
nod. One brother was set to govern Naples, another was made King
of Holland; the servility of Spain seemed to be as safe as the compliance of Leghorn, Genoa, or Antwerp. But there were three serious
gaps in the French customs line, Germany, Russia, and Portugal,

[1] Appendix II.

which could not be left unfilled without fatally wrecking the plan. Of these the widest and most important was the northern littoral of Germany, which could only be brought into the system by the acquiescence or coercion of Prussia.

The weak government of this rough and valiant people had been compelled by the Treaty of Pressburg to accept from Napoleon the electorate of Hanover, a possession of the English Crown, long coveted by the statesmen of Berlin, but only to be acquired at the cost of a breach with England. The Prussians attempted in vain to reject a gift which they could not pocket without condign punishment from the British fleet, but since the one object of his astute generosity was to embroil them with the Court of St. James, Napoleon sternly refused to vary his terms. War broke out and the expected happened. England blockaded the ports and seized the merchant ships of the reluctant brigand. In Berlin, where anti-Gallican spirit was now running high, it was thought intolerable that Prussia should be involved in a war with her natural ally at the dictation of a tyrannical alien whose large and victorious army was still menacingly cantoned in southern Germany. Napoleon took very little pains to tranquillize Prussian apprehension, and when it leaked out that in the course of some abortive negotiations with the Government of Charles James Fox, the French Emperor had actually offered to restore Hanover to England, the cup was full and Frederick William mobilized his army.

Napoleon was prepared. Though his correspondence in the summer of 1806 is mainly occupied with the affairs of Calabria, and gives the impression that he was more interested in securing Joseph in his new kingdom in Naples than in the affairs of the north, he still kept a watchful eye upon the Prussians, knowing that war might come, and that, if it came, the army of Austerlitz would be ready to meet it. When the hour struck, he confounded his enemy by a plan which ranks among the technical masterpieces of the military art. The Prussian army, which enjoyed a reputation far in excess of its real merits, was moving forward, under its aged commander the Duke of Brunswick, along the north of the Thuringian forest in the expectation that it would strike the communications or parry the attack of an army advancing from the Rhine. Had Napoleon pursued this route he would still probably have won a victory, for in numbers and calibre he was superior to his adversary; but it would have been a victory of an ordinary and inconclusive kind. The Prussians would have been driven back upon their lines of communications, and would have kept alive a defensive war until such time as they were joined by their Russian allies. But Napoleon wanted an extraordinary and crushing victory. It was not enough for him to beat the Prussians, he must cut them from their base and destroy their army. Concentrating on the Main and then swiftly advancing in a north-easterly direction through the pine-clad gorges of the forest he pushed forwards towards the Saale with 160,000 men, confident of success and overflowing with contempt for a supine and stupid opponent. The weather was superb, the countryside rich in provender, and there was hardly a straggler in the army, which marched thirty miles a day. On the evening of October 12, Davout with the third corps was at Naumberg, placed between the Prussian king and his capital, and in possession of the Prussian magazines. The disconcerting news that his position was effectually turned drove Brunswick to recommend a northerly retreat; but it was then too late to escape the storm-cloud scudding up from the south. On October 14, Napoleon fell, to his own surprise but with overpowering numbers, upon Hohenlohe's covering force at Jena. His victory was decisive; but the greater honour belongs to Davout, who, encountering the main force of the Prussians at Auerstadt, showed that a small contingent of the army of Austerlitz, undirected by the genius of Napoleon and pitted against an adversary superior to itself in infantry, cavalry, and guns, could nevertheless win a crushing victory.

This double blow administered on the same day, and followed up by a close and annihilating pursuit, placed Prussia under the heel of Napoleon. Two days before the battle he had written a letter to Frederick William III, couched in that peculiar strain of lofty eloquence which he could affect on solemn occasions, in which the Prussian king was warned of an impending defeat and urged to make peace before it was too late. When the blood had once been shed the conqueror refused to hear of an armistice. He intended so to abase the Prussians that never again should they be able to contest his authority. He besieged and took all their fortresses, made his headquarters in their capital, and levied a crushing war-contribution upon a people already exhausted by extraordinary charges. And having thus in a most signal way 'avenged the defeat of Rossbach', he issued (November 21) from Berlin the famous series of decrees which

proclaimed the British Isles to be in a state of blockade, and pro-
hibited all commerce and correspondence with them.

Before these dazzling successes could be permanently secured it
was necessary for Napoleon to fight another campaign. Though
Blücher had been forced to capitulate at Lübeck, and Hohenlohe
had laid down his arms at Prenzlau, there was still a small fragment
of the Prussian army at large, which in combination with a Russian
force advancing to its relief through Poland, might be strong enough
to repair the disaster on the Saale. Napoleon advanced to Warsaw
and attempted to bring on a decisive engagement in December;
but the enemy escaped from a net which was spread too wide, and
the actions of Pultusk and Golymin showed that the swift and
brilliant strategy of Ulm was not to be repeated amid the rigours of a
Polish winter and against the baffling obstacle of Polish mud. The
month of January was spent by the Emperor at Warsaw and enlivened
by the charms of a Polish mistress, the fair Countess Walewska, who
bore him a son, afterwards destined to be a foreign minister of France.
But pleasure did not relax his vigilance, and hearing in February that
Bennigsen was advancing to the relief of Danzig he rushed northwards to attack him. The confused and savage struggle which took
place amidst blinding snow at Prussisch-Eylau is just one of those
engagements which lend force to Tolstoy's theory that a commander
counts for nothing in a battle, and that victory is a result of forces too
multitudinous to assess. For many a French soldier who survived it,
that day of blood and snow came as the first sobering touch of
tragedy in a glorious epic of adventures. Napoleon remained upon
the field and claimed the victory; but he had lost 25,000 men and
was no further advanced towards a peace.

Against the dark background of this inconclusive campaign, with
his army demoralized by privation and shaken in battle, with the
Swedes threatening his rear, and Austrian enmity impending on his
flank, Napoleon shot out with incredible nimbleness flash after flash
of protean diplomacy. He concluded an armistice with the Swedes,
protested pacific aspirations to the Austrians, and made abortive
overtures to his two principal antagonists in the field. To create
embarrassment for the Tsar he concluded a treaty with the Shah of
Persia, and with a solemn prophecy that the hour for the regeneration
of the Ottoman Empire was at hand, earnestly exhorted the Sultan
of Turkey to fresh exertions against a common enemy. The national

patriotism of the Poles was astutely encouraged just up to the point at which it would assist the French without unduly alarming the susceptibilities of the Austrians. A grave military error on the part of Bennigsen relieved Napoleon from a situation to which every month of suspended operations would have added a fresh peril. There is a little tributary of the river Pregel which runs into the sea at Königsberg called the Alle, and in one of the curves of the Alle is the village of Friedland. Here in a bad position with the stream behind him and with a force of four to seven, the Russian general allowed himself to be caught by Napoleon. The French victory was so complete that it drove the ruler of an invulnerable empire to believe that he was seriously wounded.

The Peace of Tilsit, signed on July 8, 1807, is an arrangement reflecting an extraordinary situation rather than a profound harmony of interests between the contracting powers. A Franco-Russian alliance became a natural result of a compact and powerful Germany, and was afterwards further cemented by the common rivalry of France and Russia with England. But when Napoleon met the Tsar upon a raft on the Niemen, Germany was a mosaic of weak and warring governments, and immense tracts of space divided the most eastern outposts of the Muscovite from the British factories on the Hooghly. In the place of the Oriental antagonism of the later nineteenth century, the English and Russians in Napoleon's day were bound in a close conjunction of commerce. The foreign trade of Russia was mainly done with England, and there was no merchant in St. Petersburg whose profits would not be gravely affected if the Anglo-Russian alliance were broken off.

Apart from the erroneous conviction that nothing could be done after Friedland, Alexander was suffering from an acute state of irritation at the lukewarm support which he had received from his English allies in the recent campaign. He was therefore the more prone to accept an alliance recommended with all the seduction of Napoleon's manner, and sweetened with a prospect which might well outweigh the loss of some seaborne luxuries to the aristocracy of his capital. Among the historic passions of the Russian race none is stronger or more heartily recommended by the Greek Church than the redemption of the Byzantine Empire from the Turk. Alexander was not immune from emotions which had assailed some of the greatest of his predecessors, and when Napoleon suggested that the partition of Turkey was an object which the alliance might be able to effect, he swallowed his scruples and came to the lure.

There was a public and a private treaty. By the first Alexander recognized the changes which Napoleon had already effected, or now proposed to effect, in the political map of Europe: Prussia mutilated of its western and eastern provinces; a new kingdom of Westphalia under Jérôme Bonaparte on the one hand; a new grand-duchy of Warsaw under the King of Saxony on the other. The secret treaty was even more significant, for it prescribed the course to be pursued, should England decline to accept the mediation of Russia, or Turkey the mediation of France. In the first case Russia would join the continental blockade and combine with France in forcing Denmark, Sweden, Portugal, and Austria to make war on English commerce. In the second case Napoleon would assist the Tsar to partition the European possessions of Turkey, save Constantinople and Roumelia. The exception is a footnote to Napoleon's ambition, for when Alexander asked for the Turkish capital he was met by a stern refusal. 'Constantinople! Never! That would be the mastery of the world.'

Napoleon was in the finest spirits. The agonies and anxieties of the Polish campaign had been succeeded by banquets, courtesies, and a brilliant peace. He liked the Tsar: 'He is a very handsome, good, young Emperor, with more mind than he is generally credited with'; and in the Russian alliance he felt that he had secured the sanction and support which were necessary to rivet his dominion in the West. The Queen of Prussia, too, had pleased him, the more so that he had resisted, while enjoying, her entreaties. It was satisfactory to know that Prussia was under his heel, mutilated in territory, exhausted in treasure, and heavily burdened by a French army of occupation. He hoped, perhaps expected, that England, confounded by such triumphs, would accept the Russian terms, restore her colonial conquests, and amend her maritime law. In that event he would be free to obey the call of the East; but if the islanders were still blinded by arrogance he was now so placed that he could 'conquer the sea by the land'.

7

The Qualities of Empire

BY THIS TIME the Empire of Napoleon, though it had not yet reached its extreme measure, was far in advance of the opinions and ideals cherished by the French nation. 'The Rhine, the Alps, the Pyrenees, these', said Talleyrand to the Tsar, 'are the conquests of the French nation. The rest is the conquest of Napoleon.' And although the unbroken uniformity of his military triumphs silenced the critic and kept alive the devotion and enthusiasm of the army, the Emperor was uneasily aware of the fact that the nation was tired of war, that each successive victory evoked a diminishing response in public opinion, and that the Grand Empire rested on a basis of personal achievement rather than of national assent. When the news of Marengo came to Paris the delirium of joyful excitement surpassed belief. Six years later the intelligence of Jena hardly stirred a ripple in the pool. Mme Junot, who moved among soldiers, tells us that though the duel with England was popular, there was very little feeling for a war with Austria in 1805; and while the designs of the Emperor on the mainland were thus regarded with a growing sense of lassitude or dismay, the passion for distant enterprise over sea, which made the British Empire, was so conspicuously absent from the French temperament at that date, that the expedition to San Domingo was widely regarded as a measure devised quite as much for the chastening of the French republicans as for the due admonishment of a rebel colony.

In this essential opposition between the national interest of France and the promptings of his own ambition we find the explanation of many characteristic features of Napoleon's imperial policy. The Emperor was astute enough to see that if the principal burden of

maintaining his dominion were cast upon France the stability of his
throne would be seriously undermined. The cardinal axiom of his
Empire was accordingly to spare as far as possible the pockets of his
French subjects, and to charge the cost of his ambition to the account
of his foreign victims. It is true that some additions were made to the
financial burdens of France, and that the inconvenience of war was
indirectly brought home to the French taxpayer in the enhanced
prices of wine, salt, and tobacco. So long, however, as a nation
continues to escape any fresh imposition of direct taxation or any
serious depreciation of currency, the sharp lesson is never fully learnt
by the non-combatant section of the community. Napoleon neither
raised an income tax nor tolerated paper money, and the manu-
facturers and merchants, who are generally the first to feel the strain
of a war, were consoled by a system which threw open the markets
of Holland, Germany, and Italy to French trade without involving
a relaxation of the domestic tariff against the new dependencies of
the Empire. So far then as finance was concerned the pinch was felt
not by the wealthiest and most civilized member of the Empire,
but by the relatively poor dependencies. France was spared, while
in the Italian, German, and Dutch provinces of the Empire half the
domains were permanently appropriated to Imperial uses and the
inhabitants triply mulcted by war contributions in specie, by French
billetings, and by the obligation of finding and equipping local
contingents to the Grand Army.

The means by which Napoleon attempted to create and sustain an
Imperial feeling in France are characteristic of that mixture of the
vulgar and sublime which we find in his conversation and character.
At the end of his first Italian campaign he rebuked Marmont for
having neglected to feather his nest after the example of Masséna
and many another officer who had laid the foundations of a princely
fortune in the plunder of Italy. He was well pleased that his generals
should have a material interest in campaigning and a substantial
stake in the countries which their valour had brought under his
dominion; and with the establishment of the Empire he gave an
extended application to this principle. A number of ducal and
princely fiefs were created, mainly (though not exclusively) out of the
Venetian, Istrian, and Dalmatian provinces wrested from Austria, so
that at the most perilous angle of the Empire there might be a cluster
of military families, pledged like the frontier feudatories of the fifth

century, by urgent considerations of the pocket, to defend it. The enormous incomes showered on the marshals, and derived not from the French Exchequer but from the domains of the conquered dependencies, were similarly granted with the object of popularizing the Empire with the military caste. But the interests of the common soldier were less carefully regarded, and the victors of Jena and Friedland received part of their long arrears of pay in coin which had depreciated forty per cent.

The creation of a new nobility with large fortunes and entailed estates was a departure, far more important than the Legion of Honour, from the revolutionary principle of social equality. Napoleon defended his inconsistency by pointing out that no political privilege was associated with rank; nor would anyone accuse him of desiring to prepare an oligarchy. His motive was to range round the dynasty a circle of powerful and wealthy families, whose estates, held together under a special legal privilege, would stand out like conspicuous islands in an ocean of peasant holdings.

Another institution dating from this period, and founded in the same desire to promote Imperial conformity, is the University of France. The idea of a single corporation, comprising all branches of public instruction, from the village teacher to the university professor, and itself controlled and guided by a few cardinal and directing principles of political hygiene, is naturally seductive to that type of mind which holds that the purpose of the State cannot be too deeply graven on the nature of the citizen. Napoleon, who disbelieved in humanity without the support of a strong discipline, was greatly impressed with the work of the Catholic orders in promoting the principle of authority. 'There will', he wrote, February 15, 1805, 'be no fixed political state if there is no teaching body with fixed principles. As long as children are not taught whether they ought to be republican or monarchical, Catholic or irreligious, the State will not form a nation.' He was resolved that young France should be schooled in the military, religious, and deferential temper, after the Spartan or Jesuit example. His *lycée*, or public school, was half monastery, half barrack, its teaching staff celibate, its discipline military, its creed that wonderful Imperial catechism in which the Emperor is portrayed as the instrument of God's power and His likeness upon earth; and the *lycée* was under the University Council, which in turn was controlled by the State. Private endowments exempt the older universities and

D

schools of England from the irksome constraint of Government supervision, and they have preserved under a rule of liberty a polite and respectable convention. Napoleon's University, which was founded in 1808, endured for three generations after the fall of the Empire, and has incurred the criticism which an attempted educational monopoly naturally invites. The complete intellectual harmony of forty million Europeans is an end as hopeless of attainment as it is little to be desired, and since Napoleon did nothing for the primary schools the great mass of the people was unaffected by the loyal prescriptions of the University.

Nevertheless there is a quality of permanence in all that part of Napoleon's work which affects the organization of historic France. Here he built upon a ground-work of inherited instinct, followed the centralizing trend of national history, and obeyed the ordered genius of the Latin race. The Grand Empire was a less substantial fabric. Even where, as in Italy, it fortified deep and valuable elements of national feeling, it never lost the character of a great improvization of war, in Napoleon's own terms of 'a conquest made from England'. Boundaries were constantly changing, as if the map of Europe were a kaleidoscope shaken by a capricious hand in fits of malevolent enjoyment. Thus Holland was first a dependent republic, then a dependent monarchy, and finally, since King Louis would not adequately execute the laws of blockade, an incorporated and much tormented fragment of France. Such evidence of restlessness was well calculated to disturb the servants of the Emperor in foreign parts. The best administration is grounded on a lively hope that some part at least of the building will stand the stress of time. But how could such a hope take root in the shifting quicksands of Napoleon's diplomacy? The Constitution of Westphalia, which was far in advance of any native product, was intended to serve as a pattern to Germany, and was in fact a source of pride to the Hessians, Brunswickers, and Prussians who formed the population of that heterogeneous state. But what guarantee was forthcoming that the Westphalian Constitution would not share the fate of the Italian extinguished at the first breath of opposition; or that the Westphalians themselves would not awake some morning to find that by an Imperial decree they had been converted into Frenchmen, their constitutional kingdom at an end, and Cassel proclaimed the fourth or fifth city of Empire?

Napoleon often spoke of his realm as a federation. Now in so far as this term has a technical meaning, it implies a division of sovereignty between the national government of the federal union and the governments of the states or provinces into which that union is divided. The national government is sovereign for certain defined purposes, the state or provincial governments are sovereign for other purposes. There is an allocation of duties, a distribution of rights; there are boundaries chartered and guaranteed against aggression on either side. The spirit of a federal government is that communites sharing many distinctive qualities, traditions, and interests, but united also on a common interest, enter into a bond framed upon such nice principles of equitable compromise as to satisfy both the particularist feeling on the one hand and the larger aspiration on the other. Nor is there any feature more characteristic of a federation than its scrupulous allocation of fiscal burdens. Of all this there is nothing whatever in the Napoleonic Empire, neither a division of sovereignty, nor a circumscription of functions, nor a fair re-partition of the charges of peace and war. Finally there was no constitution. The Empire may be likened to three concentric circles—France including the annexed and incorporated provinces, the dependencies in Germany and Italy created by Napoleon (e.g. Westphalia, Berg, Italy), and those autonomous states, like Bavaria and Würtemberg, which under the articles of the Confederation of the Rhine were bound to furnish contingents for the army. It is no more an argument against Napoleon than it is against the present loose state of the British Empire,[1] that the several parts of this vast dominion were not combined in any form of legislative union; for if no account is taken of the spirit, nothing can be argued from the letter. The British Empire is cemented by common interest and common sentiment; the cohesion of its French counterpart was at once of a looser and a stricter kind, for it depended on the will of a despot and the force of an army of cosmopolitan conscripts.

The high Imperial opportunities, so far as they were extended to persons outside the civil service of France, were given to the natives of the annexed departments, and contingents from Belgium and Holland, Piedmont, Genoa, Tuscany, and Rome were dispatched to the capital of the Empire to serve on the Senate, the Legislature, or the Council of State. It was fully present to Napoleon's mind that such opportunities would educate an Imperial spirit and familiarize

[1] Written in 1912.

his new subjects with that large and constructive way of handling affairs which had now, through the pressure of his own character and intellect, become habitual with the able members of his Council. To a generation educated on a free Press and an active Parliament, a purely executive body is not the ideal seminary of public virtue. It is too apt to be composed of elderly men and to be wedded to routine. Napoleon devised a scheme for combating this inherent vice of official representation, and ordered the debates of the Council of State to be followed by a number of chosen youths, drawn from every part of the Empire, and possessed of intelligence, zeal, and a competent fortune. In the *auditeurs*, as these young persons were called, the Emperor expected to find the Imperial executive of the future.

The resemblance between the Napoleonic and the Roman Empire, though losing something of its closeness upon examination, is still the most striking analogy in political history. The autocracy, the centralization, the tribute, the auxiliaries, the two Imperial capitals crowded with the spoils of the civilized world—these are the obvious and familiar points of comparison. *Cuncta collegia praeter antiquitus constituta distraxit*, writes Suetonius of Julius Caesar, and the jealousy of free corporations which inspired the policy of Julius and his successors is deeply imprinted on the law of the French Revolution and on the Napoleonic Code. It is true that the provinces of the early Roman Empire enjoyed a degree of local liberty unknown to any French department or dependency during the Napoleonic age. Nor was the scheme of government under Diocletian and his successors as strict, as economical, nor as effective as that of Napoleon. On the other hand, the historian will note some points of analogy between the organization of the frontier provinces of the second and that of the Catalonian and Illyrian and Polish marches of the nineteenth century. So, too, in the ecclesiastical sphere, despite an enormous development of the religious life of the world, we find curious points of analogy. The worship of Rome and Augustus may be matched by the Imperial catechism made by the hand of Napoleon himself, and enjoining semi-divine honours to be paid to the office and person of the Emperor of the French. As the Roman Government presented a special sacrifice in the Temple of Jerusalem, presumably out of compliment to the religion of the Jews, so Napoleon professed the Koran in Egypt, established the Roman Catholic Church in France, and being confronted with an assembly of Dutch divines in Utrecht declared that he had been on the point of joining the Protestant Communion, and that in that case thirty or forty million men would have followed his example. The religious policy of both Empires was in the first instance characterized by a large toleration for all creeds not inconsistent with social order or due political obedience to the Government. But the ecclesiastical outlook of Napoleon was more positive than that of the pagan, more comprehensive than that of the Christian Caesars. The religious impulses of Europe had become too important to be treated with disdain or neglect, and too obstinately various in their manifestations to admit of a persecuting and exclusive preference. The French Empire, therefore, pursued the system of impartial regulation and establishment. It disciplined and controlled the Jew, the Protestant, and the Catholic, regarding the members of these communions as equal citizens of the Empire, equally and fully subject to all its burdens. Napoleon was not a religious missionary like Julian or Charlemagne, but an indifferent like Pontius Pilate. Religion was to him a useful vaccine against social distempers. If he had a mission it was to smooth over doctrinal differences, to minimize or eliminate ecclesiastical controversy, and to emphasize the distinction between secular and ecclesiastical functions. The dissidence of Dissent struck him when he first came across it in Holland with an unpleasant thrill, as highly inconvenient to the police. 'If you are against the Pope,' he said to the Jansenists, 'range yourself with the Protestants. But if you admit the power of the Pope, then respect his decisions.' It was not for a club of obscure Dutch pedants to abridge the authority of the Vicar of Christ. That necessary and salutary function belonged alone to the Emperor of the French, who represented the supreme source of civil power in Latin Christianity.

The image and name of Charlemagne, which so frequently occurs in the Imperial correspondence, was powerfully recalled to the common mind of France by the triumphant conclusion of the Marengo campaign. English visitors to Paris, during the Peace of Amiens, reported that it was the general expectation that the First Consul would shortly assume the title of Emperor of the Gauls; and if this was the common talk and feeling of Paris, we may guess with what power the example of the great Frankish hero appealed to such a mind as Napoleon's. The French Empire betrays many signs of this feeling. The sovereign who rules France and Belgium, Germany and the Spanish march, who inaugurates his Empire by a pact with the Pope of Rome, who takes the iron crown of Lombardy, carves out military fiefs for his vassals, summons an ecclesiastical council, poses as the civil head of the Catholic Church of the West, and leads a miscellaneous host drawn from every quarter of his vast Empire in an assault on the half-barbarous and wholly heretical empire of the Tsar, is he not a new Charlemagne? Modern historians have suggested other medieval analogies. Taine has found in him the Italian *condottiere*, and Masson, an almost unreserved admirer, reminds us that the hammer of the Pope, the Jesuits, and the monks, was the descendant of certain medieval Bonapartes who, like Dante, were expelled from Florence for their Ghibelline opinions.

In one respect at least the Empire of Napoleon was neither Roman nor medieval, but intensely modern. Napoleon was the genius of economy. Not Wellington, not Pitt, not Gladstone, all of them jealous husbands both of time and money, approached Napoleon in this particular of harsh, persistent, and relentless economizing. Frugal in dress, sparing in food and drink, parsimonious of time, and contemptuous of amusement, he turned his jealous and challenging eye on every franc expended in the public service. There was, we imagine, in the whole course of history, no great state managed with so scrupulous an intention of paring down all unnecessary expenses, no great state in which the officials were so ceaselessly tormented about every sixpence or sou, or where it was so impossible for any municipal body to make a free experimental and productive use of its resources. Almost immediately after the *coup d'état* of Brumaire Napoleon put down upon paper, for the benefit of his brother Lucien, then Minister of the Interior, some thoughts upon the administration of the communes of France. And in this memorandum, one of the most remarkable state papers of the time, he at once strikes the note which continues to dominate his domestic policy. The 36,000 communes of France are described as the heiresses of the feudal régime, heiresses liberated by the Revolution from the control of noble and priest, and thereupon endowed with legal personality, but so despoiled and pillaged by the bandits of the Directory that they are encumbered with debt, and unable to make an intelligent use of their new freedom and their new resources. The problem of internal government in France was therefore to conduct these helpless and diseased bodies back to a wholesome state of solvency. How this is to be done is then shown in all its successive stages. A general inventory of the 36,000 communes is to be made under nine specified headings, so that when the indebted communes and the amount of their burden have been duly ascertained, the whole weight of the administration may be focused on their relief. The prefect is to visit them twice, the sub-prefect four times a year, on pain of dismissal. The mayor who will not co-operate must go; the mayor who achieves distinction in his economies is to be rewarded by a visit to Paris, an introduction to the Consuls, and a monumental column in the village or town whose solvency he has helped to secure. Napoleon achieved his ends; a system of strict mathematical economy, uniformly impressed upon every village and town in France by the Ministry of the Interior, succeeded in effecting a great reduction of municipal debt; but when we talk of these financial triumphs, or of the military exploits of the Empire which they were designed to subserve, we must remember that the medal has another side, and that if we could revisit any great provincial town of France as it stood in any year from 1808 to 1815, we should find the schoolmasters and clergy starving upon miserable pittances, the schools empty of scholars, the public hospitals short of nurses and appliances, industry at a standstill, and the government of the town listless, incurious, and sapped of all initiative. It is not sensible or imaginative finance to lay down for the rule of the Medes and Persians that the cost of office expenses in a town is to be fifteen centimes per inhabitant. We cannot go into the reasons here, save that finance, like all human things, loses much by being treated mechanically, but such a rule is characteristic of the labour-saving appliances necessary in a great and highly centralized Empire. Being compelled to treat men as figures, such a government ends by viewing life itself as a matter of abstract arithmetic.

8

The First Check

THE EFFORT to complete the continental blockade brought Napoleon
into collision with the two strongest forces in European civilization,
the Catholic Church and the spirit of nationality. He had long
regarded the existence of a Papal state, which Catholics thought
necessary to ensure the spiritual independence of the Pope, as a
harmful anomaly in European affairs. The evil, however, had been
tolerated in the political settlement of 1797, and the Pope, who
assented to the Concordat and came to Paris for the Imperial coronation, was still the temporal ruler of a dominion stretching across
Italy from Terracina to Rimini. At whatever cost of diplomatic
friction a cool and prudent statesman would have allowed this
situation to continue, for the strength of the Pope did not lie in the
feeble government of his small and impoverished Italian principality,
but in his power of arousing the Catholic conscience of Europe.
Napoleon after Austerlitz was neither cool nor prudent; having
assumed the mantle of Charlemagne he argued that he was Lord of
Rome and that the Pope was a vassal of his Empire. A power so weak
in material resources, but so ingenious in chicane, might be safely
and properly coerced, and in the refusal of Pius VII to join in an
offensive war against England a sufficient pretext was found for
devouring his state. The formal incorporation of Rome in the French
Empire, which was deferred until May 1809, was at once answered by
a bull of excommunication against the despoiler of the Church. To
this the reply was an act of violence, encouraged, disavowed, and
upheld by Napoleon. At the dead of night the delicate old man who
had dared to defy the French Emperor was seized in the Quirinal Palace
and hastily driven away under military convoy to a prison in Savona.

Napoleon's idea of the Catholic Church was abruptly opposed to the conceptions and practices which found general favour after his fall. He thought of it as a department of the French Empire, to be most safely and conveniently governed from Paris, and of the Papacy as nothing beyond the foremost of the Imperial bishoprics. Regarding it as absurd that the College of Cardinals should be mainly recruited from Italy, he proposed that every Catholic country should have red hats proportionate to its population. It was for the Emperor to summon the Councils of the Church, to salary the Pope, and to support the spiritual energies of Catholicism with the might of his temporal arm. The archives of the Holy See were transported to Paris, and some hints were thrown out of a German Patriarchate independent of Rome. Indeed, had the Empire endured for ten more years it is possible that the Catholic communities of the American continent would have been obliged to sever their connexion with a Church so degraded and transformed.

While the quarrel with the Papacy was in full blast, and every Roman priest was raining anathemas on his head, Napoleon embarked upon the conquest of the most Catholic nation in Europe. To complete the continental blockade it was necessary that the Iberian Peninsula, and more particularly the kingdom of Portugal, should be effectively brought within the French system, and no sooner had a peace been concluded with Russia than Napoleon began to take steps for the coercion of the court of Lisbon. With this plan was ingeniously combined a project of vaster dimension and difficulty. The kingdom of Spain, under a weak, corrupt, and unpopular Government, had gone every length in its subservience to Napoleon. It had furnished him subsidies and ships, had declared war upon England at his bidding, and had been compelled to witness the destruction of its fleet in a quarrel in which no vital interest of its own was involved. But during the Prussian campaign, when it was believed in Madrid that Napoleon was about to meet a serious check, Godoy, the favourite of the Queen and the real governor of the kingdom, resolved upon a sudden stroke for liberty. A proclamation was issued for the mobilization of the Spanish army; then upon the news of Jena promptly withdrawn. It was sufficient to remind Napoleon of the fact that he could have no stable peace with the Spanish King, and to urge him forward in a policy which had floated before his mind in 1805, of dealing a final blow at that effete Bourbon stock from which France, Parma, and Naples had been so happily relieved.

In contriving the downfall of the Spanish monarchy Napoleon showed himself a true countryman of Machiavelli. There was never a plot more coldly and cleverly calculated to mystify, perplex, disarm, and overawe the opponents of a violent revolution. The first step was to demand of a penitent and frightened government a contingent of 15,000 good troops to serve upon the Danish frontier. When this exaction had been complied with, and the Spanish veterans had been safely shipped off to the inclement plain of Holstein, a secret convention was arranged at Fontainebleau on October 27, 1807, for the invasion and partition of Portgual. The true significance of this singular document lay in the fact that it gave to Napoleon an excuse for drafting French troops into Spain. The Regent of Portugal had consented under pressure to close his ports to English commerce, and had the blockade been the one object in Napoleon's mind this concession should have been sufficient to protect Portugal from attack. But Napoleon wanted a quarrel, and in the refusal of the Regent to sequestrate British merchandise he found a pretext sufficient to his purpose. Portugal then was to be invaded by a joint French and Spanish force, and when the kingdom had been duly conquered Godoy was to be rewarded by a principality in the South. The royal favourite, who had been thoroughly cowed by the exposure of his ill-timed and hostile proclamation, was only too eager to make his peace with Napoleon. Had his intelligence been equal to his cupidity he would have reflected that it was not the Emperor's way to requite evil with good, and that the false friend was not likely to be endowed with a Portuguese principality. Napoleon had accurately assessed the quality of the Spaniard. 'This mayor of the palace', he said, 'is loathed by the nation: he is the rascal who will himself open for me the gates of Spain.'

On October 18, 1807, Junot's army of the Gironde, 25,000 strong, crossed the Bidassoa on its way to Lisbon. Its operations were to be assisted by an equivalent number of Spaniards advancing on three routes, an arrangement calculated still further to denude Spain of troops at a moment when it was convenient for Napoleon that the country should be inadequately defended. The plan was that while Junot seized the fleet, royal family, and treasure at Lisbon, French troops should be drafted into Spain upon the friendly pretext of supporting the joint expedition. It would then be possible to terrify

the weak Charles IV into resignation or flight, to put down the unpopular Godoy, and to take over the kingdom, if not amid the
acclamations at least with the acquiescence of the natives.

When Junot after a march accompanied by great hardship finally
reached Lisbon on November 30, he found that the royal family had
embarked upon the British fleet and that the treasure and marine of
Portugal was beyond his reach. Still in broad outline Napoleon's
scheme of treachery appeared to prosper. Portugal was conquered.
Under the cloak of the Portuguese expedition five French armies
crossed into Spain, nominally to support their friends the Spaniards,
but really in order to pave the way to a French occupation. If there
remained in any Spanish mind a doubt as to the real intention of the
Emperor it must have been solved in February and March 1808,
when the French troops seized the four important Spanish strong-
holds, Pamplona, Barcelona, San Sebastian, and Figueras, and it was
learnt that Murat, the best cavalry leader of the Emperor, was
rapidly advancing on Madrid in the character of the Emperor's
lieutenant.

Then arose the situation up to which Napoleon had been working.
In a wild panic at the French advance, Charles IV, Maria Luisa, and
Godoy resolved on flight. They would go to Seville, thence perhaps
to America, to avoid the rigours of the Emperor and the still more
dangerous wrath of a nation whose long-stored hatred of their rule
was now envenomed by a sudden sense of its betrayal. But at Aranjuez
the fugitives were stopped by an insurrection which threatened to
spoil Napoleon's design; for the old king was forced to abdicate in
favour of his son Ferdinand, the Prince of the Asturias.

The new ruler of Spain was the darling of the nation not by reason
of any virtues which he possessed, for he was empty of charm,
intelligence, and character, but because in the imagination of his
country he stood out as the enemy of a shameful court. It would have
been simple for Ferdinand, having this immense popularity with his
countrymen, to have rallied the whole Spanish nation against the
invaders. Fortunately for Napoleon the man was a coward. Instead
of declaring war he ingeminated peace. Instead of retiring to Andal-
usia to rally the Spanish army, he came to Madrid, where a French
corps under Murat had arrived, and wrote a grovelling letter to
Napoleon. General Murat, who knew a craven when he saw one,
refused to acknowledge his title. Ferdinand trembled, felt his throne

insecure, and allowed himself to be lured to Bayonne on the pretext
that some personal conference was necessary before he could be
accepted by the Emperor as King of Spain. On the day of his arrival
he learnt that Napoleon had come to the conclusion that the House
of Bourbon should cease to reign.

'Countries full of monks like yours', said Napoleon, 'are easy to
subdue. There may be some riots, but the Spaniards will quiet down
when they see that I offer them the integrity of the boundaries of
their kingdom, a liberal constitution, and the preservation of their
religion and their national customs.'

Ferdinand proving recalcitrant it was found necessary to confront
him with his father and mother. Napoleon had extracted from
Charles IV a statement that his abdication had been made under
duress; and since the old man desired nothing better than to be quit
of care and turmoil, the plan was that he should compel his son to
resign and then himself sign a deed of abdication. A true piece of
Spanish comedy was enacted before Napoleon on May 2, in which
the characters were a sullen young prince, an angry, rheumatic old
father, and a licentious mother with the tongue and temper of a
fishwife. The king commanded his son to resign and was met with
a steady refusal; but there was an arrow left in Napoleon's quiver far
more pointed than a father's behest. Having received intelligence of
a serious revolt against the French in Madrid, Napoleon charged
the young man with complicity, and informed him that if he did not
resign that evening he would be treated as a traitor and a rebel. On
this Ferdinand, who had no desire to share the fate of the Duc
d'Enghien, wrote out an abdication, and since his father had ratified
a treaty on the previous day, resigning all his rights to the throne of
Spain to the Emperor Napoleon, the tragi-comedy of Bayonne was
brought to a successful conclusion. The vacant monarchy, after
having been refused by Louis, was accepted by Joseph Bonaparte,
while Murat, being given the choice of Portugal or Naples, wisely
determined to rule in Italy.

Napoleon afterwards acknowledged that it was the Spanish ulcer
that destroyed him. He had embarked upon the subjugation of a
country the like of which he had not yet met in his varied career.
Italy, Austria, and Germany were geographical expressions, bundles
of states swayed by no common passion and obeying the control of
governments which found neither source nor sanction in the popular

will. Spain, on the other hand, was a nation, standing aloof from other countries in a certain proud detachment and insensible to the movements which enliven and transform opinion. The breath of the French Revolution had not crossed the Pyrenees. Constitutional liberties, rights of man, religious toleration, the catchwords and conquests of French civilization, had no seduction for the Spaniard. He only saw in Napoleon the enemy of his religion, the kidnapper of his king, and the invader of his country. A spontaneous, sporadic movement, which was a lesson to all Europe, seized hold of the land and when, on June 23, Dupont's corps surrendered to a Spanish army at Bailén, Napoleon realized that he had miscalculated the difficulties of his task, and that Spain was not to be appeased by a paper constitution or to be held down by an ill-compacted army of raw recruits.

The Spanish rising was the first example of a long series of popular and national movements which ultimately shattered the Napoleonic Empire. The extreme difficulties of Spanish geography, the barrenness of the central plateau, the fact that all the mountain chains run across the line of advance from Bayonne to Cadiz, the badness and paucity of the roads, the river system, which is an obstacle not an aid to communication, these circumstances rendered Spain the ideal country in which to fight a defensive and guerrilla war. And there was another element of misfortune for Napoleon in the struggle which he had so wantonly provoked. The Peninsular War gave to the small land army of Great Britain just the theatre in which it could be most effectively employed. Instead of wasting the military strength of the country on purposeless campaigns in malarious sugar islands, the Portland Cabinet wisely resolved that the British army should act in conjunction with the native movements in Portugal and Spain. It was a momentous resolution, for while Wellesley's army gave the necessary stiffening to the valiant but ill-organized resistance of the Spanish people, the British operations were powerfully assisted by the scattered diversions of their allies. The first blow, struck at Vimiero on August 21, 1808, should have been accepted as an omen, for the thin red line under Wellesley's skilful handling routed Junot's army and cleared Portugal of the French.

Napoleon refused to read the signals. All through the war he persistently underrated the difficulties of Spanish geography, and constantly gave instructions to his lieutenants compliance with

which was physically impossible. His confidence was probably
confirmed by the brilliant results of a brief winter campaign 1808-9
when, advancing at the head of a superb army of 200,000 men, he
shattered the Spanish resistance in the north, restored King Joseph
to Madrid, and chased Sir John Moore over the plain of León to
the foot of the Galician hills. But there was no real ground for satisfaction. The Emperor would have been wise to accept the omens of
Bailén and Vimiero, and to have confined his operations to the country
north of the Ebro. As it was, his dashing intrusion committed him
to the continuance of a war which consumed his best armies,
weakened his military hold on Prussia, and gave infinite encouragement to all his enemies in Europe.

Nothing is more characteristic of Napoleon than the fact that while
the Spanish project was maturing in his brain he should have
reopened proposals to Russia both for a partition of Turkey and for
a joint expedition across the Euphrates to attack the Indian possessions of King George. He viewed Spain, with its large seaboard and
numerous harbours, as an element of marine power second only to
Italy, and therefore as likely to contribute to the downfall of England.
Cadiz was a key to Calcutta. But the Spanish revolt altered the
complexion of affairs and gave a new turn to diplomacy. The partition
of Turkey, which had been dangled before the eyes of Russia and
even of Austria, faded together with the Indian project out of the
canvas of practical politics. For Napoleon the main object was so to
refresh the alliance of Tilsit as to keep Austria quiet until such time
as he could settle his account with the wayward population of Spain.
The Tsar was invited to a conference in Germany specially arranged
to exhibit Napoleon in his new role of patron and protector of the
German princes. Alexander came to Erfurt (September 28, 1808),
his unreserved enthusiasm for Napoleon now somewhat strained
with suspicion, but nevertheless signed a secret deed promising help
should Austria be the first to draw the sword. The cracks were
plastered up for the moment, but no discerning eye could fail to
perceive that the weights and measures of Europe had altered since
Tilsit, that the Franco-Russian alliance was wearing thin, and that
while Napoleon was confronted with fresh perplexities, the Tsar,
who had made himself master of Finland and the Danubian princi-
palities, had materially advanced in power.

The most palpable result of the Spanish imbroglio was to reopen the ancient quarrel with Austria. Francis could hardly be expected to look with gentle curiosity at the dethronement of the Spanish Bourbons. There is a sense of comradeship, a kind of tacit trades union, among crowned heads which renders the misfortunes of kings especially significant and lamentable to their brethren. The art of dethronement which had been practised with success in Turin, Brunswick, Cassel, Florence, Naples, and Bayonne might receive a crowning illustration in Vienna. In the Spanish case it had been shown that neither weakness nor compliance was a safeguard against Napoleon's ambition. And if the Emperor was liable to dethrone his confederate in arms, what reason was there to think that he would spare a neutral? A new spirit began to stir in Austria, evidenced by the formation of a national militia and quickened by the tidings of the Spanish revolt. In December 1808 it was determined to take advantage of Napoleon's commitments in Spain and to declare war in the following spring. Three men were the shaping forces of the policy— the Archduke Charles, Count Stadion, and a young ambassador who had just learnt to know Napoleon in Paris, and was destined to play a large part in securing his overthrow. His name was Metternich, and seeing that for more than a generation that name stood for conservative repression in Europe, it is well to remember that Metternich's political barque was first launched on the tide of a popular and national movement.

Napoleon was now thirty-nine years of age. He had grown stout, but his health was good and his activity and endurance were as tremendous as ever. In his fierce pursuit of Sir John Moore he had crossed the Guadarrama on foot at the head of his troops in a blinding blizzard, and covered 214 miles in twelve days under a December sky and to the accompaniment of frost and snow. His ride back from Valladolid to Paris in less than six days was a feat hardly less creditable to his capacity for long bouts of swift and arduous travel. The old confidence was as high as in the golden days of Egypt. On paper his army stood at 800,000; and though 300,000 veterans were locked up in Spain, with his 'little conscripts, his name, and his long boots' he felt that he had nothing to fear from the Austrians.

Above all the long boots! If the war of 1809 failed to develop into a general struggle for the liberation of Germany the result was due to the wonderful rapidity with which Napoleon struck at the Austrians on the middle Danube and hurled them back upon Vienna before

the fire of revolt had caught hold of the north. With his capacity for
isolating the relevant issue he discerned that the spine of resistance
in central Europe was the Austrian army, and that if this could be
effectually broken a general paralysis of German and Tyrolese
patriotism would be likely to set in. Yet at the very outset of the
campaign his success was nearly compromised by the faulty dispositions of Berthier, a superb chief of the staff, but no general.
Napoleon had directed a concentration upon Ratisbon, but had added
the injunction that, should the Austrians cross the Inn before April
15 the army was to fall back upon the Lech. The first part of the
order had been partially carried out and Davout's corps had des-
cended upon Ratisbon, when, on April 16, the Archduke Charles at
the head of a powerful army 126,000 strong forced the passage of the
Isar. The situation of the French was one of the most extreme peril.
Davout was at Ratisbon, Berthier seventy-six miles away to the west
at Augsburg, and between the two main segments of the army there
was only a weak Bavarian corps at Abensberg. Had the Archduke
risen to the occasion he could have overwhelmed Davout's 60,000
men before assistance could have reached him, and then marched on
and crushed Berthier. But while the Archduke was marking time,
Napoleon was flying 'with his long boots' to the scene of action. He
had heard of the declaration of war in Paris on April 12 at eight p.m.,
and at four a.m. on the 17th was at Donauwörth and in command of
the situation. The manœuvres which he then proceeded to carry out,
though not perfect in every detail, have received the admiration of
most military critics, and were considered by Napoleon himself to be
his finest exploit in war. Ordering Davout with the left wing to fall
back and Masséna with the right wing to advance, he brought the
scattered fragments of his army together and then proceeded to crush
the enemy in detail. First the Austrian right was stunned at Abensberg, then the left was thrown back in confusion across the Isar at
Landshut. Finally Napoleon came up to the rescue of Davout, who
was struggling with the superior forces of the Archduke at Eggmühl,
and turned the fortunes of the day. The Austrians fell back upon
Ratisbon, fought an action on the following day (April 23), and then
withdrew across the Danube, damaged but not demoralized by the
loss of 50,000 lives in this extraordinary five days' campaign. It was
the victory of lightning improvisation over hesitating tactics. When
Napoleon learnt on the 18th that the Archduke after crossing the

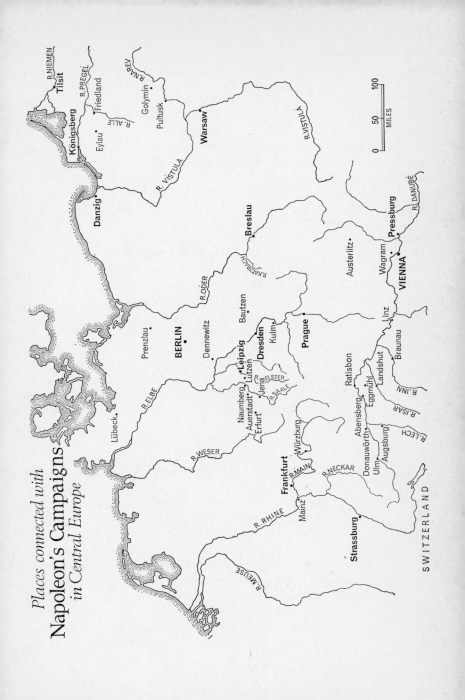

Places connected with
Napoleon's Campaigns
in Central Europe

R.NIEMEN
Tilsit
R. PREGEL
Königsberg
Friedland
R. ALLE
Eylau
Golymin
Pultusk
Danzig
Warsaw
R. VISTULA
R.NAREV

R.DANUBE
Pressburg
Breslau
Austerlitz
Wagram
VIENNA
R. ODER
R.KATZBACH
Linz
R. VISTULA

Prenzlau
BERLIN
Bautzen
Braunau
Dennewitz
Dresden
Kulm
Prague
Ratisbon
R. INN

Lübeck
R. ELBE
Naumberg
Leipzig
Lützen
Jena
R. ELSTER
R. SAALE
Abensberg
Landshut
R. ISAR
Auerstadt
Erfurt
Eggmühl
R. LECH

R. WESER
Würzburg
Donauwörth
Ulm
Augsburg

Frankfurt
R. MAIN
R. NECKAR
Mainz
R. RHINE
Strassburg
R. MEUSE

SWITZERLAND

0   50   100
MILES

Isar had deviated to the north from the straight line of advance, 'he
drew himself up, his eye glittered, and with a joy that betrayed itself
in glance, voice, and gesture, he exclaimed, "Then I have them!
Their army is lost! We shall be in Vienna in a month!"' The Emperor
was modest; three weeks afterwards he slept in the palace of Schönbrunn.

The next scene of the drama is enacted on the banks of the rushing
Danube a few miles below Vienna, where the stream is divided by
the large wooded island of Lobau. In Napoleon's own words, 'to
cross a river like the Danube in the presence of an enemy knowing the
ground thoroughly and having the sympathies of the inhabitants is
one of the most difficult military operations conceivable'. Since
Austria might gain and France would certainly lose by delay, this
most difficult operation had to be attempted. On the night of May 21,
the corps of Masséna and Lannes with the Guards and the light horse
crossed over from the island to the northern bank, and there met
with a reception calculated to quail any ordinary troops. For a whole
day 36,000 Frenchmen hung on to the villages of Aspern and Essling,
fighting desperately against superior numbers, and cut off from
support by the destruction of the bridges. On the night of the 22nd
reinforcements were sent across, but not in sufficient power to turn
the scale. After another day of fierce and indecisive combat Napoleon
withdrew his troops to the island. In the confused fighting at Aspern
and Essling he had lost Lannes, the bravest of the brave, and shown
Europe at last that he was not invincible.

The blow which finally decided the war was struck seven weeks
later in the same place, and is known to history as the battle of
Wagram. With an army greatly reinforced and exceeding that of his
adversary by twenty per cent, Napoleon crossed the Danube on the
night of July 5, and on the following day shook out his troops for a
battle. The event proved that Austrian valour was no accident, nor
French pre-eminence a necessity of nature. At the end of a fierce
struggle begun in the dawn of a July morning and sustained until
the afternoon, the Archduke Charles withdrew from the field beaten
but not broken, and leaving neither prisoner nor flag in the enemy's
hands. It was the Archduke and not the Austrian private who was
really defeated, the gunners of Napoleon rather than his infantry
who won the day. Indeed the Grand Army was no longer the splendid
instrument of earlier times. Its flower was wasting in Spain; and a

discreditable panic on the afternoon of the fight at the rumoured approach of the Archduke John exhibited the gulf which divided the young conscripts of Wagram from the tried veterans of Arcole and Austerlitz.

For the next four months a truce was observed between the two Emperors, during which either party anxiously watched the struggles which were proceeding in other parts of Europe, in the hope of some decisive declaration of fortune. The two principal dangers for Napoleon were either that Prussia should declare war, or that the Tsar, whose military support had been of the most lukewarm description, should decide to break off the unpopular alliance with France. Another but more remote peril was a grave disaster in Spain or a British descent upon the Baltic coast, so timed as to precipitate and direct the gathering volume of North German discontent. But as summer melted into autumn all these clouds passed away. The Prussians would not fight, and the Russian alliance was for the present retained by the promise of part of Galicia to be ceded by the Austrians. From the distant valley of the Tagus came the news, eagerly interpreted as most favourable to the French, that Wellesley after a battle at Talavera had retired on Portugal. And meanwhile an English expedition nominally directed against Antwerp, but allowed to waste its strength in the malarious swamps of Walcheren, served no useful purpose save to give Napoleon a pretext for raising fresh troops. Three risings in North Germany, rash, heroic, and disjointed, were crushed one by one; and with sickness breaking out in his army, Francis eventually was brought to his knees.

In the course of the negotiations Napoleon had openly hinted that Francis should abdicate the throne. 'I want to deal with a man', he said to Prince Lichtenstein, 'who has the gratitude to leave me alone for the rest of my life. Lions and elephants have often shown striking proofs of the power of sentiment upon the heart. Your master alone is not susceptible to sentiment.' It must be admitted that the Austrian Emperor, whose palace was in the occupation of his rival, fell short of the shining example of the grateful quadrupeds. In the end he was despoiled of territory carrying a population of some four million souls, and including the great harbour of Trieste and the littoral round the head of the Adriatic. And besides these material losses there was a note of ignomiy in the treaty which was signed at Vienna on October 14, 1809; for the gallant Tyrolese, who had risked everything to return to their old allegiance, were abandoned by their master to the vengeance of Napoleon.

The peace was followed at no long interval by the most remarkable political marriage in modern history. On his return to Paris Napoleon divorced Josephine and asked and obtained the hand of an Austrian Archduchess. The reason of state which governed his action was not to be deflected by the tears and entreaties of an affectionate woman whom he had once passionately adored and for whom he still cherished a tender sentiment. Josephine had borne him no children, and since the Empire demanded an heir, the obsequious Senate decreed that the marriage was dissolved, and the Bishop's Court in Paris, with a grander audacity, decided that it had never taken place at all. The choice of an appropriate substitute was for some time in the balance, and simultaneous negotiations were opened out with the courts of Vienna and St. Petersburg. In the end Napoleon decided for Marie Louise of Austria, partly because she was already of marriageable age, partly because she was a Catholic, and partly because he had experienced the reluctance and anticipated the refusal of the Russian court. When Lacuée, the Minister of War, urged in opposition that Austria was no longer a great power, Napoleon interjected, 'Then it is clear that you were not at Wagram.' It was natural to argue from the evidence of the recent campaign that the Austrian alliance would be a pillar of strength to the uncertain fabric of the French Empire. So the little Corsican adventurer married himself into the proudest house in Europe, a wedding bringing in its train a long cloud of evils, for the woman proved faithless and her country hostile, while the son of the marriage, half-Habsburg, half-Bonaparte, dragged out an empty and miserable life among the enemies of his father's name.

9

The Downfall

THE DOWNFALL of Napoleon is a trilogy of which Moscow, Leipzig, and Fontainebleau are the successive pieces and Waterloo the epilogue. Both in respect of the efforts put out and the sacrifice endured there is in this concluding struggle a sense of hugeness and desperation which has struck the imagination of posterity as exceeding the standard even of that age of blood. The powers actively engaged are more numerous, the armies are larger, the loss in battle or through privation more appalling than in any previous campaign. The casualties in the battle of the Borodino are reckoned at 80,000, the destruction at Leipzig at 120,000, and even when Napoleon had been driven back across the Rhine with the loss of hard on a million men, it cost a score of engagements to bring him to the point of abdication. That was an age before telegraphs, telephones, or railways or any energetic action of the public Press upon the mind of man. Nations were less quickly moved to wrath or suspicion. Opinion changed more slowly. It was more difficult to arouse and organize for the effective purposes of war the resentments of a people. Yet in those days of slow travel and imperfect communication the force of a single will set all Europe in movement, drove French peasants to Moscow, and drew Cossacks and Kalmucks to Paris in a collision which involved the fortunes and enlisted the passions of the ten leading peoples of the Old World.

It is a truism to point out that the moral of this titanic trilogy is the victory of the national spirit over the alien tyranny which educates and fosters its destroyer. In Spain, Russia, and England, latterly also in Prussia, Napoleon came across a force imponderable by his scales and measures, and possessing, as it proved, infinite powers of recovery and recoil. He knew the insurrection of the streets and how, as in Paris, Pavia, or Cairo, the dust could be laid by a whiff of grape-shot. It was one of his few delusions that popular movements were all of this kind, shallow, timid, easily quelled at the first show of military resolution. In Spain he judged that nothing was serious but the English army; in South Italy that a few burnings and shootings would quiet the Calabrians. In one of his letters he says lightly, 'We must denationalize Germany,' as though a great people could be drilled out of its old civilization as easily as a recruit out of his slouching ways upon parade. There is no mood if it be long sustained more dangerous to the intelligence than the imperative. The exercise of despotic power, with the crushing work which it entailed, was good neither for Napoleon's mind nor for his character. He became less amenable to advice, more irritable, more intolerant of variance, and in the succession of his Foreign Ministers, Talleyrand, Champagny, Maret, each less able and independent than the last, we have an index of the growing divergence between the policy of the Empire and the interests of France.

Napoleon's catastrophe was the logical consequence of the continental system, to the completion of which he devoted the greater part of his energy during the two years which followed the Wagram campaign. The scheme of closing the whole Continent to English and colonial goods involved not only an extended plan of conquest, but led Napoleon to incorporate in France Holland, the Hanse towns, and the Duchy of Oldenburg. But apart from the general resentment and alarm caused by these transactions, the blockade carried with it privations which came home to every household. Goethe, being a poet and a philosopher, wrote of Napoleon as a kind of apostle of the higher civilization, but if it were an inseparable part of the apostolic process that tobacco should be at famine prices, coffee and sugar unobtainable, that ships should rot in harbour, and that firm after firm should put up its shutters and discharge its hands, we may well imagine that beings less philosophical and poetical than Goethe saw nothing in Napoleon's proceedings but cruel tyranny and senseless waste. Everywhere the blockade meant loss and discomfort; in commercial communities like Holland and the grand-duchy of Berg it spelt widespread ruin. And save for the conscription, there was no feature of his policy which contributed to make Napoleon's rule so unpopular in Europe.

If the system had been executed with perfect rigour, it might perhaps have produced the desired effect. England's great wealth did not, as Napoleon erroneously believed, depend wholly upon commerce, but was in the main the fruit of her manufacturing energy. The weak spot in her economy was that her population had grown so fast that from time to time she was dependent upon continental wheat. If then all foreign supplies of cereals had been cut off from the English market it is possible that the country might have been compelled by sheer starvation to sue for peace. This course, however, was not adopted, and the French exporters were permitted under special licence to send their corn across the Channel. In view of the very considerable amount of trade done under these special licences and the great activity of the smuggler, it is not surprising that the blockade failed to achieve its end. The matter for wonder is that Napoleon should have continued to believe that by framing edicts against her merchandise, each more rigorous than the last, and all impossible of exact execution, he would be able in the end to drive England to submission.

For this among other reasons, the most important of which was his marriage, he abandoned his first intention of returning to Spain. He convinced part of his mind that with an extra turn of the commercial screw the Peninsular War would be drained at its source. In his place he sent Masséna, the ablest of his marshals, to effect the conquest of Portugal; but he neither placed him in sole command of all the French forces in Spain, nor furnished him with an adequate army, nor allowed him untrammelled freedom of action. It was given to Masséna on the heights of Bussaco, before the lines of Torres Vedras, and in his winter bivouac at Santarem, to discover what Napoleon had not even surmised, that a Portuguese army could be trained to face fire, and that in the systematic devastation of the whole country Wellington had a crushing reply to the French system of campaigning without magazines. The invasion was rolled back and Portugal was saved. In April 1811 Masséna's army recrossed the Spanish frontier, an angry, mutinous, demoralized rabble, without munitions, uniforms, or trains, having lost thirty-eight per cent of its numbers, and by its signal repulse testified to the skill of Wellington, the unwisdom of Napoleon, and to the final breakdown of the attempt to force Portugal into the ring of the continental blockade.

A more serious catastrophe threatened the scheme from the

opposite end of Europe. The development of Napoleon's policy had steadily weakened the Franco-Russian alliance. From the beginning the Tsar had felt uneasy at the harsh treatment meted out to Prussia, and at the encouragement which the creation of the grand-duchy of Warsaw afforded to the national aspirations of the Poles. He had accepted an alliance unpopular with the Russian aristocracy, still more unpopular with the Russian merchants, partly under the spell of Napoleon's personality, partly to work off a temporary irritation against England, and also in the expectation that Napoleon's friendship might serve his Oriental designs. The strain of circumstances soon wore off the gloss and revealed the seams. The Spanish revolt deferred the partition of Turkey to the Greek Kalends, and in the war of 1809 Russia, being compelled to fight Austria against the natural leaning of her sympathies, afforded a very lukewarm measure of assistance to the French. Nobody was so quick as Napoleon to discern a coming change in the atmospheric pressure of Europe. Though the Tsar was rewarded for his services in the campaign by a portion of Galicia, the greater part of that country was, under the Treaty of Vienna, presented to the Poles, to that nation of mounted swordsmen whose alliance it would be so needful for Napoleon to obtain in a Russian war. To the Chancellery of St. Petersburg this augmentation of the grand-duchy of Warsaw was full of evil omen, and Napoleon was asked for a public pledge that he would never consent to the revival of the kingdom of Poland. Such a pledge he refused to give, feeling that a war with Russia was probable, and that in that event Polish patriotism would help him to victory. Had he been without an ally on the Continent he might perhaps have walked more circumspectly, but the husband of Marie Louise felt that he was under no compulsion to trim his sails to the Russians.

All this friction need not have led to war. The breach came from the fact that, for financial reasons, it was no longer possible for Russia to adhere to the policy of the blockade. When in the middle of October 1810 Napoleon requested the Tsar to lay an embargo on all ships in Russian waters flying a neutral flag he was met by a refusal. Russia could not dispense with colonial produce, and the ships which carried it to her ports flew neutral flags. At the end of December 1810 a ukase was issued facilitating the entrance of neutral ships into Russian ports, and imposing heavy duties upon the wines and silks which formed the principal articles of French export. In this revolution of the Russian fiscal system Napoleon saw an ill-concealed declaration of hostility.

Some historians have urged that the war was inevitable, others have put the blame upon the Tsar. All wars are inevitable, if we accept as part of an inflexible order of nature the characters and actions of those who cause them. Napoleon being what he was, and the Tsar being what he was, and the circumstances of international trade and finance being what they were at that time, it is easy to show that the war must have come. In itself, however, there is nothing in the tariff revolution of another country which need bring on a war. Russia had a perfect right, finding herself saddled with a deficit, to alter her tariff in accordance with her domestic needs, and Napoleon had no right to interfere with her. The collision arose not because the Tsar was spoiling for a fight, but because Napoleon chose to regard any breach in the continental blockade as a stab to his Empire and security.

The state of Napoleon's mind in the year of preparation which preceded the Russian campaign is a conclusive proof that he had no anxiety to avoid the arbitrament of war. He thought and spoke of the coming venture not as if a real impediment to European peace had arisen which it was his painful duty to remove, but with the zest and exhilaration of a pirate at the sudden unfolding of new prospects of conquest and plunder. 'People will want to know where we are going,' he said; 'we are going to make an end of Europe, and then to throw ourselves like robbers on other robbers less daring than ourselves and become masters of India.' He began to equip expeditions for Egypt and the Cape. To Narbonne he spoke of Moscow as the half-way house to India, and of the Russian war as but the opening stage of the great triumphal progress through the East. As early as 1804 he confessed that he was weary of old Europe. He now said that in three years he would be master of the universe.

It has been brought against Napoleon's character for sane strategy that he should have seriously attempted the conquest of a country like Russia, where even more than in Spain it is true to say that small armies are beaten and large armies starve. There was, however, a contingency which had already occurred once, and might therefore not impossibly occur again, in which the stroke would succeed—a big victory near the frontier followed by a precipitate peace. Napoleon, while he spared no pains in military and diplomatic preparations, counted on the weakness of the Tsar to extricate him from the

insoluble riddle of a campaign against a desert. He misjudged the temper of his rival and found himself confronted by a strategy of evasion,
so devised as to cheat him of battle and to entice his cumbersome
army into the heart of a wilderness. In a moment of doubtful wisdom
he was pricked on to pursue, but had the Tsar listened to his overtures from Moscow, posterity would have been spared the severest
of those long military homilies which are so ceaselessly addressed to
his shade.

Whatever its shortcomings in strategy, the Russian expedition
of 1812 stands out as, up to that time, the supreme example of military tyranny in Europe. This was not a quarrel between two nations,
but a conflict between the ambition of one man and the patriotism
of a great and religious people. The French public, which was not
informed of the war until ten days after it had begun, received the
news with trained acquiescence. Napoleon was calm and serene. If he
had failed to secure the Swede and the Turk, he had taken means to
excite the enthusiasm of the Poles, and had extracted from Austria
and Prussia two serviceable contingents to guard his flanks. In the
centre he had gathered an army such as he had never yet commanded,
a miscellaneous host of over 600,000 men, recruited by methods
hardly differing from the slave raid, and two-thirds drawn, since the
best French troops were serving in Spain, from the conquered or
allied territories of the Empire. Yet this motley assemblage of Germans, Italians, Dutchmen, and Poles, marched, fought, and bled
under their French officers for Napoleon. There was neither mutiny
nor failure of persistence, and if the Grand Army of Russia perished
in its attempt, the disaster is not to be traced to the troops, but to
causes too deeply graven on the face of nature and the moral being of
man for any human tyranny, however powerful, to control them.

Napoleon's original plan was to devote two years to the campaign.
In the first he would bring the Russians to bay in Lithuania, in the
second he would advance from Smolensk to Moscow. With this
design in view he could afford to be punctilious in preparation and to
postpone the opening of hostilities till the month of June, when the
plains of Lithuania would provide fodder for his horse. If the Tsar
had waited in the entrenched camp at Drissa, which he had been
advised to prepare in foolish imitation of Wellington's lines of Torres
Vedras, the game would have been won by Napoleon. But here by a
singular paradox the French were injured and the Russians helped

by the immense superiority of the invading army. Eager as they were to try conclusions with the enemy, the Russian generals had no option but to retreat before a force more than three times as numerous as their own. Napoleon's army, 610,000 strong, which trailed behind it a commissariat proportionate to its wants, was neither successful in envelopment nor agile in pursuit; and in the middle of August the Emperor found himself at Smolensk, at the eastern end of a barren and wasted country, his army diminished by 100,000 men and with no decisive victory to his credit. There in the burning wreck of Smolensk and on the threshold of autumn he took the momentous resolve of pressing on to Moscow. He preferred to play for all or nothing rather than face an ignominious retreat or the wasting inaction of a Lithuanian winter. The Russian army under Kutusoff, the old bull-dog patriot who had at last been summoned by the nation's voice to save his country, threw itself across his path and fought the battle which Tolstoy has described in his immortal prose. The carnage of Borodino opened for Napoleon the way to Moscow, but did nothing to abate the obstinate resolve of his opponent. Kutusoff withdrew to a position not far south of the capital, from which like a bird of prey he might pounce down upon the decomposing body of the French army. The taking of Moscow, so far from helping Napoleon, only served to whet the anger of the Russians. He found a city practically bare of its inhabitants and designed to destruction by the patriotic malevolence of its governor. Fires broke out here, there, everywhere, upon a plan too comprehensive to be entirely explained by the careless torch of the plundering soldier. Yet here in a dismal mass of charred and blackened ruins he stayed till October 18, legislating for the French theatre, and hoping that Alexander would capitulate. When he began his retreat it was a full month too late, and though the snows were tardy that autumn, they were early enough to play havoc with the ragged and footsore host which sped miserably homewards before the lances of the pursuing Cossacks. When the pursuit ended on the Niemen, which was then the western frontier of the Russian Empire, more than 500,000 men of the Grand Army had disappeared.

The second part of the trilogy was played in Germany, and while it exhibits Napoleon in a grand and desperate passage of his life, forms also a notable chapter in the development of the German nation. Since one army had been completely destroyed, it was necessary if the advanced positions of the Empire were to be held to create another

in its place. With her population of thirty-six millions, France must
have contained, even allowing for the wastage of recent years, some
two and a half million men of the fighting age. But of these how many
could be raised at short notice, for a distant struggle, and with a
competent equipment? By heroic efforts Napoleon was able in the
course of four months, and without any of the modern aids to
mobilization, to put into the field in Germany 226,000 men and 457
guns; and this was accomplished at the end of an arduous and
harrowing campaign and as an item in the government of a great
Empire. This done he hurried to the front to direct operations of more
than ordinary perplexity, for in addition to the avenging army of the
Tsar, Prussia had entered the lists against him, and a reverse might
lose him the neutrality of Austria and the support of the Rhenish
Confederation.

His first two battles were empty victories. At Lutzen near Leipzig,
and again at Bautzen in Silesia, he encountered with a great
superiority of numbers a mixed force of Prussians and Russians and
failed to gain a decisive advantage. The reason must not be sought in
any obscuration of his special powers. There are signs of a fatigued
will in the later but not in the opening stages of this campaign. It is
the prime business of a general to arrive upon the field of battle with
a force superior to his adversary and to compel an engagement while
the odds are in his favour. At Lutzen and at Bautzen Napoleon
triumphantly achieved this most difficult of all operations. His eye
for ground was as quick, his gift of leadership as inspiring, as ever.
When the third corps was reeling under the attack at Lutzen he
galloped up with the young Guard behind him, a brilliant apparition,
and restored the courage of the broken troops, Indeed the mere fact
that an army of young recruits, whose sole military training had been
gained in the course of their march to the front, could be induced
to take the tremendous punishment of those two hard-fought fields
is in itself evidence of the unremitting pressure of a directing will.
The battles were indecisive simply because Napoleon was too weak
in cavalry to pursue.

Such a success was not solid. Though he had pushed the enemy
out of Saxony and Silesia and won two stricken fields, Napoleon was
conscious that without great reinforcements, especially in the cavalry
arm, he could deal no decisive blow. His marshals were tired of war,
his unripe army wasted by death, sickness, or desertion to half its

strength, his cavalry entirely insufficient. He could no longer count upon the friendship, and argued that, unless he took prompt and minatory methods, he might have to reckon with the hostility of the Austrian Empire. That power was busily arming in Bohemia, and was prepared to allow Napoleon to have peace if he would surrender his Illyrian provinces and retreat from his Polish and German conquests. Such terms were too insulting to be considered, but if an army could be brought from Italy to Laybach the Austrians might be frightened out of their insolence. With such ideas in view, Napoleon signed, on June 4, an armistice of two months at Plaswitz. It was never his intention to abandon his conquests, and if he was willing to encourage the palaver of peace it was only that he might have time to hale fresh conscripts to the slaughter-ground. The most famous passage in the memoirs of Metternich recounts how on June 26 the Austrian ambassador urged Napoleon in Dresden to accept his terms and to give peace to Europe. 'What is it you wish of me?' said the Emperor brusquely. 'That I should dishonour myself? Never— I shall know how to die but never yield an inch of territory. Your sovereigns, who are born on the throne, may get beaten twenty times and yet return to their capitals. I cannot, for I rose to power through the camp.' Metternich asked what he would do when his army of young conscripts had gone the way of the Grand Army of Russia. The Emperor grew pale and frowned. 'You are not a soldier,' he said brusquely. 'You do not know what happens in the soul of a soldier. I have grown up on battlefields, and a man such as I cares little for the life of a million men.' And as he shouted these words he threw his hat into the corner of the room. The interview lasted till the evening. As the diplomatist left the room he said to Napoleon, 'Sire, you are lost. I felt it when I came, and now that I go I am certain.'

Military critics have generally condemned the armistice on the ground that though it enabled Napoleon to call up reinforcements, it was still more useful to his enemies. When hostilities reopened in August, Austria and Sweden were in bond with the allied sovereigns, and if the Spanish and Italian armies be taken into account, Napoleon had some 700,000 men to pit against the 860,000 of his adversaries. Whether this result should have been foreseen by any prudent commander in Napoleon's position in the month of June is a matter which may admit of discussion. What is certain is, that when the war was renewed the complexion of affairs had become far less favourable to his chances; for while the mass of his fresh troops was raw and unseasoned, his enemies were more numerous, better compacted, and no less resolute than before.

Dresden, the Saxon capital, stands on the Elbe, twenty miles north of the mountain frontier of Bohemia. Here Napoleon decided to take his station, not only as part of a general plan to defend the line of the Elbe, but also that he might retain the loyalty of his Saxon and the confidence of his Polish allies. Posted at this convenient centre he calculated that he could meet the converging attacks of the three allied armies which were advancing respectively from Bohemia, Silesia, and Brandenburg. But he was afterwards brought to acknowledge that his election was unfortunate, and that Dresden was too near the mountains to enable an army retreating on Bohemia to be properly cut to pieces before it had reached the refuge of intricate and intractable ground.

And indeed the Dresden period was marked by a long catalogue of misfortunes. It had been arranged among the Allies to avoid, if possible, a serious collision with Napoleon himself, but to attack his lieutenants with vigour whenever they were to be found. This policy was almost uniformly successful. The contingents of Oudinot and Ney successively dispatched to meet the Army of the North tasted defeat at Gross Beeren and Dennewitz, battles which are memorable in the military annals of Prussia as definitely marking the resurgence of her glory. At the eastern extremity of the wide field of war, Blücher, commanding the army of Silesia, beat Macdonald on the Katzbach. The one exception to this significant list of reverses was afforded by the earliest battle fought after the resumption of hostilities. The advance of the Bohemian army upon Dresden on August 22 was prompted by the confident expectation that while Napoleon was occupied against Blücher in Silesia, the place, which was but slightly fortified, would be taken before he could return to defend it. The event showed the falseness of these calculations. Schwarzenberg was as slow to advance as Napoleon was quick to return, and in the great battle fought outside the walls of Dresden the defence had the advantage of the Emperor's inspiring direction. After two days' fighting, August 26 and 27, the Bohemian army was repelled towards the frontier; and had the victory been followed up with the old energy, Dresden would have ranked with Jena as one of Napoleon's decisive victories. History is, however, full of examples of great events affected or determined by little accidents of physical health and fitness. In the early stages of the movement Napoleon had shown his accustomed flexibility, swiftness, and resolve. He had brought the Guards back into Dresden at the rate of ninety miles in seventy-two hours, and on the first day of the battle, by a masterly economy of his reserves, had repulsed 150,000 men with less than half the number. On the second day the French attack, though the Emperor had received strong reinforcements during the night, was delivered with less than the accustomed vigour; and the Austrian centre was still unbroken when at five o'clock in the evening Schwarzenberg, learning of the rout of his left, determined to retire. Then it was that Napoleon, had he been in the full tide of his energies, would have pressed on in a desolating and remorseless pursuit. The army of Bohemia was the main army of the Allies, composed of Austrians, Russians, and Prussians, and accompanied by the three sovereigns of those countries. The effect upon Europe of its destruction would be incalculable, and to destroy it should have been the main objective of the campaign. By a combination of fortune and skill Napoleon had succeeded after a heavy engagement in driving Schwarzenberg to retreat, and he should have spared no pains in converting the retreat into a rout and the rout into a capitulation. But rain fell in torrents on the 27th, and Napoleon, after five days in the saddle, was chilled and exhausted. When the enemy began to give way he considered that his work was over, sent for his horse, and, the rain dripping from his grey overcoat, rode back to Dresden. At seven o'clock he wrote to Berthier that the enemy was not in retreat, and that everything led him to believe that a great battle would take place on the next day. Even when the morrow had proved this prediction to be false the pursuit was relinquished to lieutenants, and while Vandamme's corps, which had been sent to cut off the enemy, was itself enveloped and destroyed at Kulm, Napoleon was quietly resting in Dresden.

By the middle of September the French army in Saxony had been worn down from 400,000 to 250,000 men. Desertion was rife, the hospitals were filling, and the difficulties of commissariat, especially after Ney's defeat on September 6, increased with alarming rapidity. The only hope of success lay in the unlikely case that one of the allied armies would allow itself to be caught and destroyed by Napoleon before the other two could come to its assistance. For a month the

Emperor marched and counter-marched, with Dresden as his pivot, fatiguing himself and his army in the vain but necessary attempt to bring on an engagement. A palsy of indecision seemed to come over him. He could not resolve upon a bold retreat. Eventually his hand was forced by the action of the Allies. In the last week of September Blücher broke out of Silesia, crossed the Elbe, joined hands (October 7) with the Prusso-Swedish army under Bernadotte, curving down from the north upon Napoleon's line of retreat to France, as Schwarzenberg, debouching from the Bohemian mountains, slowly circled round from the south to meet him. The first plan which occurred to Napoleon, as he became aware of this enveloping movement, was to send Murat to Leipzig to hold Schwarzenberg, while the main body of the army under his own direction essayed to bring destruction upon Blücher. But it soon became apparent that Blücher was not to be caught. The plan was therefore reversed, and on October 12, after some days of agonized perplexity, Napoleon resolved to join forces with Murat and to defeat the Bohemian army marching up from the south before Blücher and Bernadotte came to its assistance. At noon on October 14 the Emperor rode into Leipzig. On the morning of the 16th his army was concentrated for battle.

The battle of Leipzig is one of those engagements in which an army of fixed numbers is pitted against an enemy which receives reinforcement after reinforcement after the battle begins, and eventually wins an overwhelming victory by reason of these successive additions to its mass. Napoleon began the battle with 190,000 men against 200,000, and had therefore on the first day, and especially in the early hours of the first day, a real chance of success. Had he concentrated on Leipzig, as he might well have done, in time to fight Schwarzenberg upon the 15th, he would have met an army markedly inferior to his own, because its concentration was not yet complete, and would probably have won a victory. Or again, his chance would have been greatly improved if he had not chosen to leave 30,000 men under St. Cyr in Dresden, a step against which he had himself tabulated a list of cogent objections. Still, despite the depression of energy and incoherence of plans which had marked the earlier stages of his westward movement he had, once his mind was clear (October 12), outpaced the Austrians and brought his men upon the field with a touch of the old velocity; but in one vital particular his calculations were mistaken. While in the villages south of Leipzig the battle was raging against Schwarzenberg, a dull boom of guns was suddenly heard to the north of the town. Napoleon galloped to the spot and found that Marmont was engaged with Blücher. The old Prussian had marched rapidly on Leipzig from the north-west and began to hammer at the French positions with such vigour that it was impossible for Napoleon to withdraw a man for those crucial operations against Schwarzenberg, from which he expected, and not without reason, to establish a decisive advantage.

It was a day of desperate fighting and memorable carnage; but when night fell Napoleon was a beaten man. He had failed to crush the Bohemian centre, or indeed to break at one point the circle of his foes. While his own losses were irreparable, Schwarzenberg received strong reinforcements during the afternoon. In such a situation an indecisive action was equivalent to defeat, and a prudent general would have lost no time in extricating his army from a position which every hour of delay would make more desperate. But to the dismayed surprise of his best subordinates Napoleon issued no order for retirement. On the next day, a wet Sunday, he lay in his bivouac and sent a letter to the Austrian Emperor proposing an armistice, and vaguely hinting at concessions. But his enemies knew that he was at last in their toils, and did not mean to be cheated of their prey. The overtures were spurned, and when the battle broke out again on the 18th, all the Austrian reserves were up, and Bernadotte had marched in with 65,000 men to help Blücher on the northern side.

Encircled by overwhelming forces but yet disputing every inch of the ground, the French were steadily pushed back upon Leipzig. At four p.m. the Emperor gave orders for retreat, and all that night the French troops were crowding back into the town so that they might cross the Elster on the following morning. The next day the rout began and the great river of fugitives pressed onwards, in indescribable confusion, towards and over the solitary bridge. Here some time after nine o'clcock General Chateau met a man 'in a peculiar dress' standing in a little group. He looked like a burgher, and for all that he was deep in thought was whistling '*Malbrouk s'en va-t-en guerre*'. It was the Emperor, and as he calmly whistled that old air the torment of his shattered army swept onwards before his eyes.

There was nothing to be done after Leipzig but to capitulate to the conquerors, for at that central shock the whole fabric of the Empire came crumbling to the ground. All Germany rose to throw off the

E

yoke of Napoleon; even the Bavarians, suddenly exchanging alliance for hostility, contested his retreat. Holland declared for the House of Orange, Naples made a treaty with Austria, the dream of a French kingdom in Spain utterly vanished as Wellington steadily drove Soult across the Pyrenees. In France the desire for peace was passionate and universal. The wealthy and intelligent classes of the nation had for many years viewed the course of Napoleon with anxious and disapproving eyes, and now that two great armies had been destroyed in as many years, that industry was at a standstill, the treasury empty, and the country menaced by foreign invasion, the curse of political servitude came home to every thinking man with poignant force. Strong as was the Imperial feeling with the mass of the peasantry and the army, the reflecting part of the nation had now surrendered to liberal ideas. It wanted peace with honour and the national control of national policy. The Legislature, a body of ordinary but representative middle-class men, boldly expressed its distrust of the Government and desire for constitutional liberty. Napoleon suppressed the audacious assembly with a violent rebuke; but a signal had been given to the Allied Powers that France and Napoleon were no longer in unison.

There is a type of character which rejects the thought and evidence of humiliation. In his cool moments Napoleon recognized that the Confederation of the Rhine was a 'bad calculation', the continental system 'a chimera', and the Grand Empire a lost splendour never to be retrieved; but his pride refused to accept the award of his intellect. 'Do you wish', he said to his Council of State, 'to descend from the height to which I have raised France, to become a simple monarchy again instead of a proud Empire?' He could not bear to leave France weaker than he had made or found her; and as he thought of the defection of his allies a convulsion of rage would seize him and he vowed revenge. 'Munich', he cried, 'must burn, and burn it shall.' Even if he were compelled to capitulate he did not intend to swallow his humiliation for long. In two years' time he would be in arms again; but so long as there was a chance of success in the field he would avoid the abasement of a treaty, trusting to the military errors of his opponents, to the defection of Austria, and to the insurgent valour of an invaded nation. His plan was to temporize in diplomacy, so that to the French people he might appear as proffering peace, while he seized every occasion of punishing the enemy.

It was this inflexibility of temper which proved his ruin. It was no part of the original policy of the Allies to demand Napoleon's abdication or a change of dynasty. From Frankfurt (November 1813) they sent an envoy to Paris offering to treat, if he would accept as a basis the natural frontiers of France, the Rhine, the Alps, and the Pyrenees; and later on (February 4, 1814), after France had been invaded and the defence had suffered its first important defeat, he could have kept his throne by the surrender of Belgium and Savoy and acquiescence in the frontiers of the old monarchy. Apart from the counsels of personal prudence there was a plain call of patriotic duty to conclude a peace.

There was a moment after the defeat of La Rothière when he seemed resolved to accept the inevitable, for, on February 4, he gave Caulaincourt *carte blanche* to treat with the Allies; but on the following morning he was found stretched out upon the floor sticking pins into a map. In the night he had heard that the allies had divided forces, and that while Schwarzenberg with the main army was marching on Paris by the southern route of the Seine, Blücher with his smaller force of Prussians had struck north into the valley of the Marne. When Maret appeared to get his signature for the ambassador's instructions he saw the gleam of battle in his master's eye. 'I mean to beat Blücher,' said the Emperor; but although the soldier's judgement was confirmed by three brilliant victories, that business of beating Blücher lost Napoleon the throne of France.

Napoleon's defensive campaign in the valleys of the Seine and the Marne has been justly admired as an example of how a small force, brilliantly and resourcefully handled, may, when acting on interior lines, inflict blow after blow upon an enemy superior in numbers but suffering under the evils of a divided command. The quick dash from Troyes after Blücher, the three swift blows (Champaubert, Montmirail, Vauchamps) which headed off the Prussian advance along the Marne, then the dart southwards to the Seine and the victory over the southern vanguard at Montereau, such exploits (February 10–17) were sufficient to show that the master had lost none of his daemonic craft. Yet these victories, though for a time they arrested the advance of the enemy, were not sufficient to decide the campaign. One at least of Napoleon's enemies was determined, come what might, to struggle through to Paris. Blücher was no genius, but a rough, coarse, illiterate soldier with a patriotic heart burning to avenge the wrongs of Prussia. While dismay reigned in the Austrian camp the old Prussian was as stout as ever. He was not one to accept defeat. On the contrary, he again pushed for the north-west, joined a Prusso-Russian force marching from Belgium under Bülow, and so reinforced repelled Napoleon at Craonne and Laon. He was then in a position either to advance upon Paris or to join the southern army. He elected for the latter course, and while Napoleon was retreating eastwards to make war upon the enemy's communications, he came into collision at Arcis-sur-Aube with the main body of his enemies. Thirty thousand men half dead with fatigue cannot beat a hundred thousand who are comparatively fresh. Napoleon was repulsed, but nevertheless for a few days persevered in his easterly march. We may marvel at his infinite resource. Some critics hold that no course was so promising as that which he shaped for himself in the days immediately preceding and following the battle of Arcis, since by collecting the scattered garrisons of Alsace and Lorraine he could have gathered a formidable army with which to break the communications and promote the division of the Allies. However this may be, the plan was abandoned; and hearing that the invaders were marching on Paris, Napoleon determined to fight his last battle before the capital. But the enemy had three days' start, and before Napoleon could throw himself into the city, Paris had capitulated to the Tsar.

Thus headed off from the capital of the country, he repaired to the castle of Fontainebleau, eager, did the marshals support him, to continue the struggle against the peace of Europe and the solid interests of France. But the marshals were tired of the desperate cause and anxious to secure their fortunes before it was too late. Posterity will hardly condemn these valiant and faithful men for advising abdication, seeing that it was demanded by the sovereigns, enacted by the Senate, and agreeable to the opinion of Paris. They hoped at least that the Emperor might be permitted to resign in favour of his son, and that the Napoleonic dynasty might still continue to rule in France. But the Tsar, whose ear had been gained by Talleyrand for the Bourbons, ended by demanding unconditional surrender, and the marshals accepted a decision which they had tried to influence but were unable to overthrow. On April 6 they pressed their reluctant master to write out a deed renouncing the thrones of of France and Italy, and five days later a treaty was signed, awarding to Napoleon the sovereignty of Elba, a bodyguard, and an income. There is a legend, which history dissolves, that on the eve of his departure from Fontainebleau he took poison. Such ignoble despair was no part of a character schooled in the myriad chances of fate. Even in this hour of deep humiliation he felt that his destiny was not yet accomplished. 'I shall always', he said, 'be an extraordinary man.' But meanwhile, as he drove southwards through royalist Provence with a storm of curses round his ears, a certain cynical, inglorious, and very gouty old gentleman who had been quietly residing in a pleasant country house among the fat pastures of Buckinghamshire was preparing to take up the government of France.

10

The Last Phase

THE NEXT EPISODE of Napoleon's life is the most wonderful adventure in history. After ten months of active government in his miniature kingdom he suddenly stole across the sea and landed with 1,200 men upon the coast of France. Avoiding the hot royalism of Provence, he struck across mountain paths to Grenoble, and eventually, without a battle or a skirmish, without a shot exchanged or a drop of blood spilt, drove into Paris and resumed the government of the country. The troops which had been sent out to resist his advance were won over by the simple magic of his presence. When the men of the fifth regiment barred the defile of Laffray he came into their midst opening his grey overcoat and invited them to fire. 'Soldiers,' he said, 'you can shoot. Do you not recognize me as your Emperor? Am I not your old general? It is not ambition which brings me among you. The forty-five best heads of the government of Paris have called me from Elba, and my return is supported by the three first powers of Europe.' The falsehoods were not perceived. Delirious enthusiasm greeted him along his route. Had he been the father of his people, crowned with long years of beneficent endeavour to ease the economic pressure on the poor, he could not have received a more glowing welcome. The recollection of the war-taxes and the blockade and the holocaust of lives seemed suddenly to be blotted out. All sorts and conditions of men were fascinated by his address. He got out of his carriage to embrace an old republican blacksmith, cross-questioned a schoolboy on local history, spoke to a scholar of his interest in the translation of Strabo, to the lawyers of a contemplated reformation of the Codes. As the news of his victorious progress trickled into Paris, angry confidence passed by swift stages to anxiety, dismay, and despair; so that when on the wet evening of March 20 Napoleon's carriage clattered up to the Tuileries, the old king and his retinue were far away and the city was abandoned to the servants of the Empire.

The miracle is not to be explained by any deep-laid conspiracy. Napoleon escaped from Elba because he had within him a fund of unexpended energy which the petty activities of his tiny realm could not satisfy; and he succeeded in reaching Paris because two classes of men, the soldiers and the peasants, wished to see the Bourbon Government handsomely chastised. The monarchy of Louis XVIII was neither corrupt nor tyrannical. It stood for peace and retrenchment, and permitted under the forms of a written constitution a far larger measure of political and civil liberty than had ever been enjoyed under the rule of Napoleon. No one could rightly accuse it of being malevolent, or as likely to interfere with the material progress of the country. But being from the first without any deep root of national support, it had irritated patriotic sentiment by a series of injudicious measures. In particular it had offended the army by a harsh and extreme policy of retrenchment, and the peasants by the expectations which it had encouraged that the land-settlement of the revolution would be shortly reversed.

Against an obscurantist government conducted by a royalist clique Napoleon shone out as the hero of the Revolution. Every peasant knew that the Little Corporal would not require him to disgorge the lands which before the troubles had belonged to the seigneur and the abbot, and that whatever drawbacks might be attendant upon his rule, there was at least no fear of priest or *émigré* under Napoleon. He was the son of the people, who could talk their language and read their hearts. His image was known in every cottage; his victories were recounted again and again by every fireside. He was already, like Charlemagne of old, a part of the national legend, called by quaint, endearing nicknames, and the theme of innumerable anecdotes. Of her new rulers, on the contrary, France knew little, save that for five-and-twenty years they had lived in exile protesting against the achievements of the Revolution and estranged from the glories of the Empire. Despite all the eloquence of Chateaubriand, since Rousseau the greatest master of French romantic prose, the old dynasty could not strike the imagination of the country. Some hated it for what it had been; others despised it for what it was; the majority feared it

for what it might become. The Charter might be safe under Louis
XVIII, but the Comte d'Artois, his brother and heir, was a narrow
bigot, whose political creed was autocracy only tempered by subservience to the most intolerant section of his Church.

In this suspicious and irritated mood of the public mind Napoleon
found his opportunity. As he proceeded through France he spoke the
language now of the Jacobin, now of the liberal, suiting his words
to the character of his audience; to the peasants offering himself as a
shield against feudal and clerical reaction; to the bourgeois as a retired
and penitent conqueror whose mind was filled with thoughts of
liberty and peace. Finding that nothing was so generally apprehended
as a renewal of the war, he painted himself as a man who had doubt-
less made some mistakes of ambition, but was not essentially wedded
either to a career of foreign conquest or to a policy of domestic
repression. Throughout his public life his ultimate ideal had been the
pacific federation of Europe under the guiding influence of France.
He represented that he could not fairly be judged by institutions
which had been framed in the torment and stress of war, or by a policy
the harshness of which was the necessary result of transitional circumstances. He had hoped to make France mistress of Europe, but had
been taught by calamity that his ambition, in which he was not alone,
was overstrained. But part of his unfulfilled programme could still
be executed and he would now proceed to give to France those free
institutions which had hitherto been postponed through the exigen-
cies of war. With these professions on his lips he induced Carnot,
the staunch republican, to accept the portfolio of the Interior, and
summoned Benjamin Constant, the leading liberal publicist of the
day, to draft a constitution.

If the Empire could really have been made compatible with liberty
and peace, the French people could have had no government better
suited to their needs. Long after Napoleon's death, the Church, the
Codes, the University substantially remained as the great architect
had left them, and French society was Napoleonic under rulers who
violently rejected the Imperial claim. The shadow which obscured
Napoleon's glory was the suspicion which had steadily grown to an
awful certainty, that war and despotism were inseparable and in-
grained parts of his nature. To efface this impression was now clearly
the first call of prudence, and Napoleon resolved to invest his new
liberalism with the sanction of a national *plébiscite* and the solemnity

of a ceremonial acceptance in Paris. On June 1, amid a great con-
course summoned to the Champs de Mars, the Emperor swore to
obey the new constitution, which had enacted liberty of the Press,
responsibility of ministers, and parliamentary government. But forms
and ceremonies cannot alter facts. A liberal chamber could never
durably coexist with Napoleon, and though for the moment the
Acte Additionnel was accepted, it was the Emperor's intention, as he
observed at St. Helena, at once to dismiss the Chambers in the event
of a victorious campaign.

The expectation, if it were ever seriously entertained, that Europe,
having squandered years of painful effort upon the conquest of
Napoleon, would now passively acquiesce in his return, was swiftly
and peremptorily dispelled. No sooner had the news of his escape
reached Vienna than the plenipotentiaries of the eight leading powers
there assembled declared him an outlaw, and soon afterwards Great
Britain, Russia, Austria, and Prussia bound themselves each to put
150,000 men into the field and to keep them under arms 'until
Bonaparte should have been rendered absolutely incapable of stirring
up further trouble'. Nevertheless Napoleon was not without hope
that he might detach Austria and England from the ring of his
enemies. He knew that extreme tension over the destinies of Poland
and Saxony had arisen at the Congress of Vienna between Prussia
and Russia on the one hand, and Austria, England, and France on the
other, and though the question had been adjusted, he might reasonably
expect that the feeling of resentment and suspicion would remain.
To Austria, therefore, and Great Britain he addressed letters protesting his desire to keep the peace and his acquiescence in the restricted
frontiers of France. His word was not accepted by either ruler.
Indeed, had there ever been a chance that Austria would alter her
mind, that chance was dispelled in April, when Joachim Murat,
acting on his own initiative, broke out of Naples and invaded the
Papal states, calling upon the Italian nation to revolt and to accept
him as king of a united Italy.

The issue between Napoleon and Europe was fought out in
Belgium. Here was gathered the vanguard of the Allies, a miscellaneous host of English, Dutch, Belgians, and Germans under the
Duke of Wellington, and the more homogeneous Prussian army of
which Blücher was the nerve and Gneisenau the brain. It was inevitable that Napoleon should seek out his enemy in Belgium, even if by

so doing he was compelled to act with an inferior force. To have
waited in the heart of France till all the allied armies had crossed the
frontier would have been unwise from a military and disastrous from
a political point of view. It was clearly the best chance for Napoleon
to defeat the Prussians and the English before the great hosts of
Austria and Russia were ready to take the field. His striking force, it
is true, when the necessary deductions had been made for an insurrection in the Vendée and the defence of the frontiers, was hardly
more than half the combined numbers of the enemy; but it was an
army of veterans, as well schooled and as highly tempered as any
that Napoleon had commanded, and it was no rash calculation that
with such an instrument he could defeat the enemy in detail, annex
the Netherlands, and so recover the wavering confidence of France.
Proclamations dated from Brussels were duly prepared in expectation
of victory.

These proclamations were never issued. Yet even if the Waterloo
campaign had been won by Napoleon, he could not have averted the
inevitable catastrophe. The total mass of the allied armies, of which
the forces stationed in Belgium were but a fraction, was some
800,000 men, and behind them were the illimitable reserves of an
indignant continent. The temper of Europe was such that even if
France had retained the hot zeal of the early Revolution, and Napoleon the matchless vigour of his youth, the war must have gone
against him. But times had changed, and in the year of Waterloo,
France (save for her small regular army) was a disenchanted nation
and Napoleon an altered man, still wonderful in energy and resource,
but less confident, less drastic, less continuously efficient than before.
The old lavish tributes of men were not to be extracted from a
country where the current of middle-class opinion was pronouncedly
in favour of peace and liberty; and a hastily levied militia of sailors and
gendarmes, national guards and customs officers, was no sufficient
support to a regular army, which all Napoleon's efforts had not been
able to increase by more than 84,000 men. The battle of Waterloo,
then, is not one of the decisive battles of the world in the sense that
had the issue been other than it was, history would have been greatly
changed. Before a shot had been fired, Napoleon was a beaten man.
Yet the battle is justly celebrated not only as the one occasion in
which Napoleon was pitted against the great British master of infantry warfare, but as marking the end of the French ascendancy in

Europe and the close of that long struggle between the armed doctrine
of the Revolution and the aristocratic and ecclesiastical traditions
bequeathed from the feudal age.

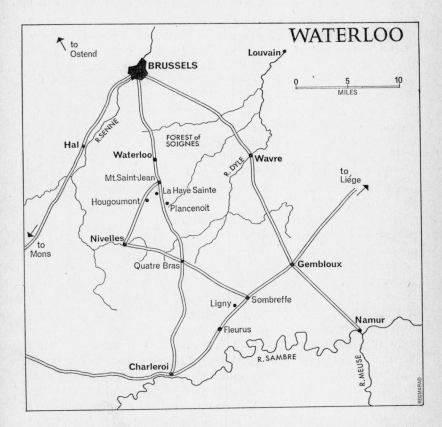

The central factor in the Waterloo campaign is the overwhelming
numerical superiority of the Allies. A French victory was impossible
against the conjoined forces of Blücher and Wellington. It was
therefore Napoleon's plan to cut through the centre of the long
Anglo-Prussian cordon, which was strung out on the Belgian frontier, and to destroy whichever of the two armies might first cross his
path. The early stages in the development of this design were marked
by speed, secrecy, and precision, and by the evening of June 14 the

French army was concentrated in the neighbourhood of Charleroi, while yet the English and Prussian forces were scattered over a front of a hundred miles, extending from Liége to Ghent. Here, however, a delay occurred which, though not fatal to Napoleon's chances of success, was of immense value to his enemies. The passage of the Sambre, which should have been accomplished by the early afternoon of the 15th, dragged on until the middle of the following day, so that when Napoleon was ready to join battle on the 16th, the alarm had been given and the English and Prussian armies were rapidly drawing together to contest his advance. By noon of the 16th, Blücher had concentrated three out of his four army corps (some 90,000 men) at Ligny, while Wellington was hurrying up reinforcements to the defensible position of Quatre Bras, lying some six miles west of the Prussian lines on the Brussels–Charleroi road. Moreover, on that morning the Duke had met the Prussian commander and had promised to march to his assistance provided that he were not attacked himself.

It is a mark of a great general so to dispose the movements of his troops as to be able rapidly to adapt himself to any one of the many possible emergencies which may arise. When Napoleon returned to his quarters at Charleroi at eight p.m. on the evening of the 15th, overcome with fatigue after seventeen hours in the saddle, he had the satisfaction of knowing that he had forced the passage of the Sambre and pushed back the Prussian outposts of Zieten's corps which had been sent to screen the allied position. Beyond this he had no certain knowledge, save that the four Prussian army corps were widely dispersed and unlikely to be collected in time for a battle on the following day. Accordingly he split his army into two divisions, giving the left wing to Ney and the right to Grouchy, and himself commanding a reserve capable of reinforcing the left or right as the situation should demand. Orders were sent to Ney to hold himself ready to push on towards Brussels by the Charleroi road, while the right wing was instructed to march on Fleurus and to attack any Prussians who might be found there. It was the Emperor's expectation that while the Prussians could not oppose more than 40,000 men to Grouchy's advance, Ney would find very little difficulty in brushing aside the easterly posts of the Anglo-Dutch army. The situation would then develop itself in the most flattering manner. After the exposed Prussian corps had been crushed at Fleurus by the superior numbers of the French, the Emperor would strike westwards to the assistance of Ney, enter Brussels on the morning of the 17th, and then proceed to annihilate the composite army of the Duke of Wellington.

Completely as this reckoning was upset by the rapidity of Blücher's concentration, Napoleon's plans were so laid that they could be adjusted with even higher chances of success to the new conditions. Finding himself unexpectedly confronted at Ligny not with a fraction but with the main body of the Prussian army—not with 40,000 men but with 90,000—he made up his mind to envelop and destroy his enemy by summoning Ney, or some part at least of Ney's force, to leave the Brussels road and to sweep down upon the Prussian flank and rear. Meanwhile with his 60,000 men he would engage the Prussians, containing their left or easterly wing and briskly attacking their right and centre. The action began at three o'clock. 'It is possible', said the Emperor to Gérard, 'that three hours hence the fate of the war may be decided. If Ney executes my orders properly not a single gun will escape him.'

The field of Ligny, which was the last of Napoleon's victories, and one of the fiercest in a long catalogue of savage encounters, practically decided the campaign. At ten o'clock, when the last shots were exchanged, the Prussians had withdrawn from their positions 'damnably mauled', as the Duke of Wellington had predicted they would be, but still an organized force capable of executing a compact and orderly retreat. At the extreme end of the day, by letting loose the Guard at the Prussian centre, Napoleon had driven the enemy from the field but he had not gained his crushing victory. Owing to a long array of blunders he had been obliged to fight without the help of a single man from Ney's command. That brave and spirited officer, who for all his staff was compelled to rely upon a single aide-de-camp, had advanced along the Brussels road with a natural but calamitous deliberation. When he might have carried the Quatre Bras position at nine o'clock, or even as late as eleven in the morning—for the Prince of Orange had but 7,800 men and fourteen guns to defend it—he postponed operations till the afternoon, and found to his cost that he was faced with an enemy already reinforced and destined before nightfall to be increased to fourfold its original strength. Ney, therefore, was too hotly engaged at Quatre Bras to do more than prevent Wellington from helping Blücher. Yet there was a factor in the

situation which, had it been utilized, might have given Napoleon that
complete victory over the Prussian army which was needed to decide
the campaign. The Corps d'Armée of d'Erlon, 20,000 strong,
belonged to Ney's command, and was tardily marching on Quatre
Bras, when at 4.15 p.m. an aide-de-camp rode up from Napoleon
with written directions that it should forthwith proceed to Ligny.
The four divisions turned eastwards and were already visible to
Napoleon, though in an unexpected quarter, when a hot order from
Ney demanded an instant return to Quatre Bras. With a singular lack
of judgement d'Erlon obeyed his immediate superior, and this force
of 20,000 men, which might have given a decisive finish to either
engagement, marched and countermarched between the two battlefields without striking a blow.

Up to this point Napoleon's conduct of the campaign had been
marked by singular decision and brilliance. He had surprised his
enemies by the speed and secrecy of his advance, had cut in at the
weak point of junction between the hostile armies, and had driven
off the Prussians with the loss of 15,000 men. If Blücher had not been
permanently crushed at Ligny, the result was largely due to causes
beyond the Emperor's control, to the imperfect co-operation of Ney's
divisions, to the error of d'Erlon, and to the bad staff-work in both
wings of the army. But on the morning of the 17th, Napoleon fell
into a mistake which was just as serious as Ney's dilatory advance on
Quatre Bras or as d'Erlon's absence from the field of Ligny. He
came to the conclusion, grounded on some fatal mixture of optimism,
indisposition, and fatigue, but on no serious probing of the facts,
that the Prussians had been finally put out of action and were streaming eastwards in dire confusion away from Wellington and down their
own line of communications through Namur and Liége. His movements were accordingly characterized by some hours of leisurely,
perhaps fatal, confidence. He drove round the battlefield, talked
Paris politics with his generals, even contemplated resting his army
for the day. It was not until noon that he issued his final instructions
to Grouchy to follow up the Prussians with 33,000 men and ninety-
six guns, nor did he himself join hands with Ney at Quatre Bras until
two in the afternoon. Had he effected this march four hours earlier
he could have attacked the Duke of Wellington, always assuming
that the Duke had awaited his attack, with an advantage of two to one.
As it was he was hardly in time to annoy a retreat which was power-

fully assisted by torrents of rain and by the skilful handling of the British cavalry.[1]

On that drenching Saturday night the Duke took up his station on the Mont Saint-Jean, a low eminence eleven miles south of Brussels, which his fine eye had already selected as appropriate to his methods of defence. Opposite him, at a distance of 1,300 yards, a ridge known as La Belle Alliance, from the name of a farm on its crest, was receiving all through the night successive increments of the weary and famished army of Napoleon. In numbers and weight of artillery the advantage lay with the Emperor, who could oppose 246 guns to 184, and an army of 74,000 French veterans to the 67,700 men, of whom 24,000 only were British, who made up the miscellaneous and disjointed host of the Duke of Wellington.

The decision to defend the Mont Saint-Jean position was taken upon the assurance of Prussian help. Early in the morning of the 17th Wellington had been apprised that the Prussians were retreating, not eastwards as Napoleon imagined, but northwards in the direction of Wavre, a village which lies some thirteen miles from the field of Waterloo. To the officer who brought him this intelligence the Duke replied that if he could hope to be supported even by a single Prussian corps he would wait for Napoleon at the Mont Saint-Jean and give him battle. Otherwise he would be compelled to sacrifice Brussels and to retreat beyond the Scheldt. A message which reached the British headquarters late on Saturday evening clinched the case for an immediate battle. Blücher's army was concentrated at Wavre and the Duke might count on its assistance. Even allowing for muddy cross roads, it was no extravagant calculation that somewhere about noon the Prussian guns could open upon the French right and begin to ease the strain upon the British position.

Wellington's then was the waiting, Napoleon's the forcing game. The whole problem of British tactics was to defend the ridge of Mont Saint-Jean until the arrival of that single Prussian corps which Wellington expected, and had with his habitual exactitude of measurement asserted to be the indispensable condition of success. Yet in a battle where everything depended on the time-table, Napoleon waited until thirty-five minutes past eleven in the morning to begin the attack. The delay was explained partly by the late

[1] Wellington was apprised of Ligny at 7.30 a.m. Napoleon, who had heard nothing from Ney, could, after such a battle, hardly have moved before 8 a.m.

arrival of some of the French contingents, partly by the state of the ground, which was reported to be too sodden after the recent rains to admit of the easy movement of guns and cavalry. Still it can hardly be doubted that whatever weight might properly be attached to these considerations, Napoleon would not have scrupled to defy them had he surmised that 90,000 Prussians were collected within four hours' march and with the full intention of joining hands with Wellington during the course of the day. Though he had received a message from Grouchy at two a.m. that the mass of Prussians seemed to be marching on Wavre, nothing was further from his mind than the possibility that his operations would be seriously embarrassed by Blücher. He thought of the Prussian army as a broken and dispirited force, perhaps 40,000 strong, divided into two streams of fugitives, one of which was pouring eastwards towards Liége and the other northwards towards Brussels. At ten a.m. he sent a message to Grouchy to attack the Prussians at Wavre, and even when at one o'clock he had ascertained that Bülow's corps was in sight, he was not seriously alarmed. It was, he thought, but a single unsupported body, some 30,000 strong, which, if Grouchy moved rapidly from Gembloux, would be caught between two fires and annihilated. 'This morning', he said to Soult, 'we had ninety odds in our favour. We have still sixty against forty.'

With that optimism which is the natural complement of courage and resource, but which is sometimes also the ally of a headstrong judgement, Napoleon took a low view of Wellington and his men. 'I tell you', he said to Soult, who, having tasted English quality in the Spanish wars, regretted the detachment of so large a force under Grouchy, 'that Wellington is a bad general and that his army is a bad army.' Nor would he believe Reille, another Spanish veteran, who urged that the British infantry was impregnable to direct attack and only to be vanquished by manœuvres. He determined to employ against the thin red line the shock tactics which had served him on so many a field and had recently been crowned with success at Ligny, to pierce the British centre by a grand frontal attack delivered after a shattering cannonade from his massed artillery. The operation was to be assisted by a diversion, not to be too severely pressed, upon the farm of Hougoumont, which lay a little in advance of the British right. Sitting at a little table with his maps before him he anticipated that his sixtieth pitched battle would be a glorious day.

In bare outline the battle of Waterloo takes the form of a series of tremendous charges delivered at the left and right centre of the British position supported by a concentrated fire from the guns, and repelled by the steadiness of the English and German troops. In the execution of these famous attacks there appear to have been two important faults from which Napoleon may with some probability be absolved. The great charge of d'Erlon's division which opened the central attack at one o'clock was made in four columns each of so narrow a front and great a depth (seeing that the column was composed of eight battalions ranged one behind another) that while offering an admirable target to the British infantry, it possessed an altogether inadequate power of reply. It was, however, Napoleon's custom to leave the minor tactics to the discretion of his subordinates; and the vicious formation of d'Erlon's charge may be classed as one of those mistakes for which the lieutenant is more properly responsible than his chief. The other error was even more serious, for it conditioned all subsequent stages of the fight. At 3.30 p.m., when the British infantry was still unshaken, Ney dashed across the valley, if the shallow depression between these two ridges can so be called, at the head of an immense body of horse to attack it. Then began a long succession of furious cavalry charges, which spent themselves in vain against the solid valour of the British and German squares. That the first charge was premature and insufficiently supported is certain, and those for whom Napoleon's word is as impeccable as his tactics, believe that it was undertaken without the Emperor's authority.

The battle was won by the skill and courage of Wellington, by the imperturbable steadiness of his English and German troops, and finally by the advance of the Prussians who began to affect Napoleon's dispositions soon after four p.m., and in the last hour of daylight converted a repulse into a rout. With greater activity Grouchy might have delayed but could not have arrested the Prussian advance. Blücher could have contained him and yet had two divisions to spare for Wellington. If a handful of cavalry had been told off to follow the retreat from Ligny instead of a whole division, or if the Old Guard had been sent in earlier and at full strength at Waterloo, would the result have been otherwise? It is possible, but we can never know. Perhaps Napoleon made mistakes but his brain seems to have been as clear and active as ever, and though he appears to have been unwell on the morning of the 17th, his physical achievement

during the campaign would, in any other man, have been deemed
extraordinary. On Waterloo Sunday he rose at one a.m., went the
round of his outposts, returned at three a.m., listened to the reports
of his scouts and spies, dictated fresh orders, and at nine a.m. rode
out to the battlefield. There he remained till nightfall, attending to
the course of operations and issuing orders efficiently, directly,
ceaselessly. When the army was broken beyond repair he tried vainly
to rally the fugitives, and rode onwards till he reached Charleville
at five o'clock on the following morning. In the four critical days of
the campaign he had hardly taken twenty hours' rest, and had spent
more than thirty-seven hours in the saddle.

It is also characteristic of his indomitable spirit that even after
Waterloo he continued to battle against fate. From Philippeville he
wrote to his brother Joseph, arguing that 300,000 men could still be
gathered, and that with constancy and courage all might yet be
saved. In the bulletin which he composed for the *Moniteur* on June 19
he painted the disaster as the result of an inexplicable panic superven-
ing in the moment of victory. When he arrived in Paris on June 21
his first thought was of a dictatorship to be conferred by the Chambers for the salvation of the country; but he was no longer the man
of Brumaire, and when both houses firmly demanded his immediate
abdication, he was too broken to resist. The deed was signed on
June 22. A few days longer he remained in Paris, balancing in his
mind as the ragged mob cheered him at the Élysée, whether he would
not appeal to the Jacobin spirit and stir the furies of a civil war. But
the deep Imperial instinct, which made him contemptuous of the
canaille, saved him from so dishonourable a close, and in his retreat
at Malmaison his thoughts began to turn to a new life in America
dedicated to literary work. On June 25 he wrote a farewell address
to the French army, striking in his clear and ringing prose notes of
high confidence and manly pathos which belong to the sublime pages
of literature. Then, four days later, as Blücher's Prussians were
reported in the neighbourhood he made his way towards the sea. The
Provisional Government had abruptly refused his offer to serve
France as a general under their command.

Finding at last that the land was unsafe and the sea beset by
English cruisers, he made a virtue of necessity, and in his old *bravura*
manner wrote a letter to the Prince Regent of England, announcing
that 'he came like Themistocles to seat himself at the hearth of the

British people', and to claim the protection of their laws. The reader
of historical memoirs may regret that a career so variously and brilliantly tinted should not have found a diverting close among the solid
squires of England or in the robust and equally unfamiliar air of the
American Republic. But having a general duty to the peace of Europe
as well as a special obligation to the Allies, the British Government
was compelled to see that Napoleon should never again fill the world
with the roar of his cannon. He was sent to a storm-swept rock in the
far Atlantic, and there on May 5, 1821—

> Seen like some rare treasure galleon
> Hull down with masts against the Western hues,

after a long and painful illness bravely borne, finally expiated that
deep offence of which we must seek the original root in the quarrel
between the French Revolution and the ancient society of Europe.
Three months older than Wellington, he was at the time of his
death in his fifty-second year.

Everybody must wish that he had fallen at Waterloo, charging at
the head of his Old Guard, as the dusk of evening stole across the
summer sky. Yet the St. Helena captivity, while it exhibits the violent
and paltry side of a blended character, is barren neither of historical
significance nor of intellectual grandeur. The career of Napoleon
was not closed when he stepped on board the *Bellerophon*, nor even
when he landed on the quay of Jamestown. He had still a policy to
pursue and a part to play. 'The battle of Waterloo', he said, 'will be
as dangerous to the liberties of Europe as the battle of Philippi was
dangerous to the liberties of Rome;' and in the dark reaction which
he rightly anticipated as likely to follow from the triumph of the
monarchs he descried a gleam of hope for the little boy whom he
had proudly entitled the King of Rome. Some day France would
rise against a dynasty imposed on her by foreign armies and favour-
ing an obsolete society and an outworn creed; and when that epoch
of liberal upheaval came, Frenchmen would remember the Empire,
a government popular in origin, modern in character, and surrounded by an aureole of incomparable glory. So in his conversations
and memoirs he developed those elements of his life and policy
which seemed likely to commend themselves to a liberal age, dictat-
ing accounts of the early campaigns in Italy, Egypt, and Syria, when
he laid the foundations of his renown in the service of a republic,

and representing himself in talk as the constant friend of peace, freedom, and national rights. Such was his political legacy, subtly compounded of truth and falsehood, but conceived in the spirit of a coming age. Living upon its wealth, the nephew of Napoleon rose upon the forty-sixth anniversary of Austerlitz to be Emperor of the French, and afterwards to be one of the makers of United Italy.

'I am a fragment of rock launched into space.' In this image of a meteor flashing from the unknown Napoleon depicts his irresponsible flight through history. As he turned an admiring gaze upon his extraordinary career he thought of himself not as a creature treading the narrow pathway of human convention, but as some elemental force of nature without love or hate let loose upon the world and ruled by the law of its own inner necessity. Small men strung their lives on a steady thread of principle, waiting on second-hand theories, and respected the moral prudence of the race. They were 'ideologues', trammelled by the scruples of an intellectual caste. Great men acted like a flash of lightning. It was a part of their greatness to move onwards with an easy confidence, to be exempt from the common pain and labour of decision, and even in the gravest determinations to be unconscious of the exercise of will. 'In the strong man everything is at one and the same time reason and movement. He wills with impetuosity what he has conceived with deep reflection and his heroism is all of a single piece.' Napoleon's career was marvellous, but it is even more wonderful that he often thought of it as inevitable, as the automatic response of the clear head and true judgement to the shifting stress and strain of circumstance.

The diamonds which were found sewn into a coat in his carriage after Waterloo are typical of the spirit in which he carried on his great adventure, for even in his hours of established authority and splendour he was uneasily aware that he was skirting the edge of ruin. Everyone is familiar with the story of how even as Emperor he would steal out of his palace in disguise at cockcrow to chatter with workmen and shopkeepers and so feel the pulse of the town. Power never brought false security or lulled the quick sense of peril which comes with a life spent among elemental things. To the end he was the corsair, watchful against his enemies and scenting the faintest breath of treachery in the wind.

Books have been filled with the record of his kindly actions and gracious words, for where ambition did not conflict, he could be full of amiability and pleasant helpfulness. He shed blood freely but never wantonly, using as much severity as the occasion seemed to demand, but keeping his standard of severity high. As a young general he consented, though with visible reluctance, to the shooting of 2,500 Turkish prisoners who had surrendered to his officers under pledge that their lives would be spared, a course which has been defended even in modern times by a barbarous casuistry, on the ground that the prisoners could neither be trusted if released, nor fed if retained. Later on the practice of war made him callous to slaughter, and after surveying the hideous carnage of Borodino he wrote that it was 'the finest battlefield' which he had yet seen.[1] Very different was Wellington's comment on the soldier's life. 'I hope to God', he said to Lady Shelley just after Waterloo, 'that I have fought my last battle. It is a bad thing to be always fighting. While in the thick of it I am too much occupied to feel anything; but it is wretched just after. It is quite impossible to think of glory. Both mind and feelings are exhausted. I am wretched even in the moment of victory, and I always say that next to a battle lost the greatest misery is a battle gained.'

Though he made some devoted friends and retained to a wonderful degree the capacity for frank and good-humoured intercourse with all sorts and conditions of men, Napoleon was never to be depended on for taste, truth, or charity. Nor can he be held up as a pattern of the domestic virtues. The catalogue of his amours, which were pursued sometimes without decorum, generally without sentiment, yet never to the detriment of business, is sufficient to show that he was neither above nor below the current standards of his time and calling. Yet if he was no purist in morality, he was no slave of the senses; and since the days of St. Louis French policy has never been held so high above the corrupting taint of favouritism and intrigue. In a world of struggling and greedy parvenus, stoical ambition, severe and inexorable, stood at the wheel of affairs.

His heart thrilled to the appeal of great open spaces, to the mysterious sound of the sea, to the serene charm of pure starlit skies. The little unobtrusive beauties of nature, the poise or tint of a flower, the song of a bird, the winter tracery of a tree were unnoticed, and, if noticed, would have been dismissed, like the plays of Racine, as

---

[1] *'C'est le champ de bataille le plus beau que j'ai encore vu.'* From a letter in the possession of Lord Crawford which I have generously been allowed to read and to quote.

elegancies fit only for young people. It was essential to his idea of
beauty that it should have grandeur, and to his notion of grandeur
that it should exalt the character and steel the will to high resolves.
The free play of thought, the wit, the gaiety, the elastic spirit of
invention, the love of beauty for beauty's sake—all these essential
ingredients in the life and progress of art did not affect him. 'Ah,
good taste, there is one of your classical phrases which I do not adopt.
What is called style, good or bad, hardly strikes me. I am only sensible
to the power of thought.' So his criteria in literature and art were
those not of the aesthete but of the practical man, who judges a novel
by its plot and characters, a picture by its moral rather than its
technique. 'A bad subject,' he remarked of David's *Thermopylæ*;
'after all Leonidas was turned.' Why should a painter go out of his
way to immortalize the defeat of an indifferent general? It was the
province of art and literature to reward merit and decorate success.

Nevertheless it would be untrue to say either that the grand things
in literature meant nothing to Napoleon, or that he was incapable of
himself producing literature of value. The man who remarked to the
Theophilanthropists, a somewhat absurd and pedantic sect: 'Do you
want sublimity? Well, then, read the Lord's Prayer,' was clearly alive
to the appeal of grave and simple beauty. Some of his own bulletins,
written just after the excitement of battle, are splendid specimens of
crisp and nervous French, softened here and there with a deft touch
of poetic imagination, or ennobled by a burst of real eloquence.
Refined critics, to whose tribunal he did not appeal, have often
caught a false ring in the rhetoric, and condemned the melodrama
as cheap and tawdry; but it must be remembered that in his bulletins
and proclamations Napoleon was not addressing the burgess in the
black coat, but the soldiers and the people of France. 'The men who
have changed the universe', he observed, 'have never succeeded by
capturing the leaders, but always by moving the masses'; and the
Napoleonic writings were addressed to the masses. Never was so
brilliant a fugue upon the twin themes of patriotism and glory
addressed to the multitude of any country. Like the philosophy of
Rousseau which it temporarily displaced, the literature of Napoleon
belongs to the library of the demagogue. He was the prince of
journalists, the father of war correspondents, and in the art of
engineering political opinion through the machinery of the Press he,
the tyrannical censor of newspapers, is the pioneer of those great

newspaper trusts which now impress their violent unwisdom on a suffering age.

Talleyrand, a severe critic since he had injuries to avenge, said that Napoleon's judgement, when unhurried, was excellent, and that in a life crowded with incident he was guilty of only three serious blunders in political prudence—Spain, the Pope, and Russia. If the scrutiny of modern historians prolongs the list of errors, it cannot refuse admiration to the tact for circumstance which in peace and war solved so many problems, vanquished so many dangers, and again and again turned defeat into victory. Still the question remains and may be debated with an infinite variety of qualifying phrases, how far the ultimate end of Napoleon's activity was consistent with true nobility of character. Conquest for conquest's sake is the ideal of a savage. Before conquest or empire can be justified, the end for which wars are fought and empires are won must be established in the court of moral pleas. In ultimate analysis what dream can well be more vulgar and barbarous than the conquest of the world by the sword? Apart from the bloodshed, misery, and desolation immediately involved in the process, what good or valuable result can be obtained from the general abasement of national self-respect, or the violent destruction of national individuality? Napoleon did not argue the question. He took glory as his end, found it in conquest, and was too often prone to measure it by destruction. So with the grandest intellectual endowments ever vouchsafed to man, and despite many splendid services to law, to administration, to the moral and intellectual progress of France, he remains the great modern example of that reckless and defiant insolence which formed the matter of ancient tragedy and is at war with the harmonies of human life.

APPENDIX 1

Some Maxims of Napoleon

POWER IS NEVER RIDICULOUS.

Love of country is the first virtue of civilized man.

The true wisdom of nations is experience.

High tragedy is the school of great men. It is the duty of sovereigns to encourage and spread it. Tragedy warms the soul, raises the heart, can and ought to create heroes.

Men are like figures, which only acquire value in virtue of their position.

The heart of a statesman should be in his head.

Be clear and all the rest will follow.

The vice of our modern institutions is that they have nothing which appeals to the imagination. Man can only be governed through imagination. Without it he is a brute.

Extracts! a pitiable method! Young people have time to read long books and the imagination to seize all the great things.

History paints the human heart.

Love is the occupation of the idle man, the distraction of the warrior, the stumbling block of the sovereign.

Conscription is the eternal root of a nation, purifying its morality and framing all its habits.

Education and history, these are the great enemies of true religion.

I do not see in religion the mystery of the incarnation but the mystery of the social order. It attaches to heaven an idea of equality which prevents the rich man from being massacred by the poor.

Unity of command is the first necessity of war.

I regard myself as probably the most daring man in war who has ever existed.

The first quality of a commander-in-chief is a cool head.

I have always loved analysis, and were I to fall seriously in love I would dissect my love piece by piece. Why? and How? are useful questions one cannot too frequently ask oneself.

Heart! How the devil do you know what your heart is? It is a bit of you crossed by a big vein in which the blood goes quicker when you run.

The virtue and magic of an aristocracy consist in time and antiquity, the only things I was unable to create.

A general who does great things must possess civil qualities. It is because he is reputed to be the best brain that the soldier obeys and respects him.

All the ills and curses which can afflict mankind come from London.

A great captain ought to say to himself several times a day: If the enemy appear on my front, my right, or my left, what should I do? If he finds himself embarrassed, he is ill posted.

England would have finally been no more than an appendix to my France. Nature has designed her to be a French island like Oléron or Corsica.

A constitution without an aristocracy is a ball lost in the air.

Aristocracy always exists. Destroy it in the nobility, it removes itself immediately to the rich and powerful houses of the middle class. Destroy it in these, it survives and takes refuge with the leaders of the workshops and the people.

Work is my element. I am born and built for work. I have known the limits of my legs. I have known the limits of my eyes. I have never known the limits of my work.

I had the taste for foundation, not the taste for property. My property consisted in glory and celebrity. There are only two nations, East and West. France, England, Spain, have very much the same morals, the same religion, the same ideas.

He lies too much. One may very well lie sometimes, but always is too much.

Bleeding enters into the combinations of political medicine.

I had long meditated the project of forming in France twenty or twenty-five military districts, each with its own army.

Love! I don't quite know what that means in politics.

Your letter is too clever. Cleverness is not wanted in war. What is wanted is accuracy, character, and simplicity.

Religion is an important affair in a public institution for the education of young ladies. Let them be brought up to believe and not to reason.

I regard savants and intellectuals as coquettes. See them and talk to them, but do not marry the one or make a minister of the other.

In government, never retrace your steps.

There are men fit to translate a poem who are incapable of leading fifteen men.

There is a complaint that we have no literature; it is the fault of the Minister of the Interior.

When a king is said to be a kind man, the reign is a failure.

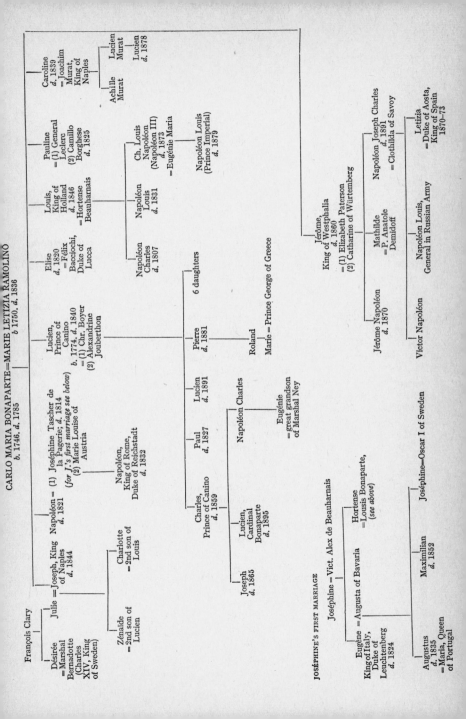

CARLO MARIA BONAPARTE=MARIE LETIZIA RAMOLINO
b 1746, d. 1785   b 1750, d. 1836

François Clary

Désirée   Julie == Joseph, King   Napoléon = (1) Joséphine Tascher de   Lucien, Prince of   Elise   Louis,   Pauline   Caroline
= Marshal   of Naples   d. 1821   la Pagerie; d. 1814   Canino   d. 1820   King of   = (1) General   d. 1839
Bernadotte   d. 1844   (for J.'s first marriage see below)   b. 1774, d. 1840   =Félix   Holland   Leclerc   = Joachim
(Charles   (2) Marie Louise of   = (1) Chr. Boyer   Bacciochi,   d. 1846   (2) Camillo   Murat,
XIV, King   Austria   (2) Alexandrine   Duke of   =Hortense   Borghese   King of
of Sweden)   Jouberthon   Lucca   Beauharnais   d. 1825   Naples

Zénaïde   Charlotte   Napoléon,   Napoléon   Napoléon   Ch. Louis   Achille   Lucien
= 2nd son   = 2nd son   King of Rome,   Charles   Louis   Napoléon (Napoléon III)   Murat   Murat
of Lucien   of Louis   Duke of Reichstadt   d. 1807   d. 1831   d. 1873   Lucien
                                        d. 1832   = Eugénie Maria   d. 1878

        Charles, Prince of Canino   6 daughters   Napoléon Louis
        d. 1859   (Prince Imperial)
                                                                                                d. 1879

        Lucien, Cardinal   Pierre   Paul   Lucien
        Bonaparte   d. 1881   d. 1827   d. 1891   Jérôme,
        d. 1895   King of Westphalia
                Roland   Napoléon Charles   d. 1860
        Joseph   Marie = Prince George of Greece   = (1) Elizabeth Paterson   Napoléon Joseph Charles
        d. 1865   (2) Catharine of Würtemberg   d. 1891
                        Eugénie   = Clothilda of Savoy
                        = great grandson   Jérôme Napoléon   Mathilde
                        of Marshal Ney   d. 1870   = P. Anatole   Letizia
                                                        Demidoff   = Duke of Aosta,
                                        Victor Napoléon   Napoléon Louis,   King of Spain
                                                        General in Russian Army   1870–73

(see above)
(see below)

JOSÉPHINE'S FIRST MARRIAGE

Joséphine = Vict. Alex de Beauharnais

Eugène = Augusta of Bavaria   Hortense
King of Italy,   = Lousis Bonaparte,
Duke of   (see above)
Leuchtenberg
d. 1824

Augustus   Maximilian   Joséphine = Oscar I of Sweden
d. 1835   d. 1852
= Maria, Queen
of Portugal

Bibliography

The vast number of books and articles on Napoleon continues to grow yearly—witness the *Revue des Études Napoléoniennes* and the *Bibliographie Annuelle de l'Histoire de France*. This list is intended merely to serve as a brief guide to further reading, primarily in English (and published in London, unless otherwise specified; books in French were published in Paris).

The fine *Napoléon* by G. Lefebvre (1953; 2 vols. trans. 1969) is rightly termed 'masterly' by F. M. H. Markham in his brief *Napoleon and the Awakening of Europe* (1954). See also Markham's *Napoleon* (1963) and J. M. Thompson, *Napoleon Bonaparte, his Rise and Fall* (Oxford, 1951), neither of which, however, entirely displaces the older *Life of Napoleon I* by J. H. Rose (2 vols., revised ed. 1934). H. Butterfield, *Napoleon* (1939) is an interesting short essay, and L. Madelin, *Histoire du Consulat et l'Empire* (1937–54) a large-scale (16 vols.) study.

Thompson made extensive use of the 32-vols. *Correspondance de Napoléon I* (1858–69), a vital source albeit 'edited'—on this point see p. 71 of the discerning survey of changing views of Napoleon by P. Geyl, *Napoleon, for and against* (1949). From some 41,000 letters printed in the *Correspondance*, its *Supplément* (1887), and other subsequent publications, J. M. Thompson includes 300 in *Napoleon's Letters* (1934). J. E. Howard, *Letters and Documents of Napoleon*, (1961–), vol. I *1784–1802* is a fuller collection in English, while J. C. Herold provides a most interesting translated selection from his written and spoken words in *The Mind of Napoleon* (New York, 1955).

Scores of contemporaries wrote their memoirs—and publicists 'ghosted' or invented some others. F. Masson, *Napoleon at Home* (2 vols., 1894) made great use of contemporaries' accounts to produce a colourful picture of the Emperor's working day, and J. Savant, *Napoleon in his Time* (1958) provides a somewhat hostile selection of passages from similar sources. Not, of course, that all Frenchmen loved the general—see Geyl, op. cit., and the extracts in J. Tulard, *L'Anti-Napoléon; la légende noire de l'Empereur* (1965); and certainly many foreigners tended not to— see A. Broadley, *Napoleon in Caricature* (2 vols., 1911).

Of the memoirs (and those marked with an asterisk have been translated, even if in an incomplete form; the dates are those of good French editions) those by the duchesse d'Abrantès* (1893) and the comtesse de Rémusat* (1905–6) are useful for Napoleon's private life—but are often unreliable even if entertaining. Roederer's notes (1909) for 1799–1806 and Mollien's memoirs (1898) are more sober and especially useful for civil activity. The Emperor's character comes through clearly in Chaptal (1893) and in Caulaincourt* (1933)—the latter as valuable for the collapse of 1812–14 as are Gourgaud* (1899), Las Cases* (1951), Montholon* (1847), and Bertrand* (1949–59) for the years on St. Helena.

On this last theme R. Korngold, *The Last Years of Napoleon* (1960) was able to use material not available to Lord Rosebery for his perspicacious *Napoleon, the Last Phase* (1904).

On St. Helena Napoleon fought his last campaign, via Las Cases and his other companions. The Emperor had always taken care to present a favourable 'image' to contemporaries—see R. Holtman, *Napoleonic Propaganda* (Baton Rouge, 1950); and now he was concerned to influence posterity— see J. Lucas-Dubreton, *Le Culte de Napoléon 1815–48* (1960). His first great campaign, though, was of course that in Italy—see G. Ferrero, *The Gamble; Bonaparte in Italy 1796–97* (1939)—and his second an unsuccessful venture into the Near East—see J. C. Herold, *Bonaparte in Egypt* (1963). Thereafter Napoleon's preoccupations embraced 'imperial' as well as merely military strategy. For the latter D. Chandler's comprehensive survey *The Campaigns of Napoleon* (1967) is very useful. For two defeats the Emperor suffered see E. E. Y. Hales, *Revolution and Papacy 1769–1846* (1960) and E. Tarlé, *Napoleon's Invasion of Russia 1812* (1942). For other preoccupations see H. A. L. Fisher, *Studies in Napoleonic Statesmanship; Germany* (Oxford, 1903); H. C. Deutsch, *The Genesis of Napoleonic Imperialism* (Harvard, 1938); H. Butterfield, *The Peace Tactics of Napoleon 1806–08* (Cambridge, 1929); J. Driault, *La Politique Orientale de Napoléon 1806–08* (1904) and his *Napoléon en Italie 1800–12* (1906); A. Fugier, *Napoléon et l'Espagne 1799–1808* (2 vols., 1930).

Fuller guides to further reading may be found, in particular, in the books by Lefebvre and Markham (1963), in the periodic bulletins published in the *Revue Historique*—see vols. 196 (1946), 205 (1951), 213 (1955), 221 (1959), 227–8 (1962), 236 (1966), 237 (1967)—and in J. Godechot, *L'Europe et l'Amérique à l'époque napoléonienne* (1967).

MAURICE HUTT

Index

WITHDRAWN